WANG GUNGWU

The **Institute of Southeast Asian Studies (ISEAS)** was established as an autonomous organization in 1968. It is a regional centre dedicated to the study of socio-political, security and economic trends and developments in Southeast Asia and its wider geostrategic and economic environment. The Institute's research programmes are the Regional Economic Studies (RES, including ASEAN and APEC), Regional Strategic and Political Studies (RSPS), and Regional Social and Cultural Studies (RSCS).

ISEAS Publishing, an established academic press, has issued more than 2,000 books and journals. It is the largest scholarly publisher of research about Southeast Asia from within the region. ISEAS Publishing works with many other academic and trade publishers and distributors to disseminate important research and analyses from and about Southeast Asia to the rest of the world.

WANG GUNGWU

JUNZI
SCHOLAR-GENTLEMAN

IN CONVERSATION WITH
ASAD-UL IQBAL LATIF

ISEAS

INSTITUTE OF SOUTHEAST ASIAN STUDIES
Singapore

First published in Singapore in 2010 by ISEAS Publishing
Institute of Southeast Asian Studies
30 Heng Mui Keng Terrace
Pasir Panjang
Singapore 119614

E-mail: publish@iseas.edu.sg
Website: http://bookshop.iseas.edu.sg

The responsibility for facts and opinions in this publication rests exclusively with the authors and their interpretations do not necessarily reflect the views or the policy of the publisher or its supporters.

ISEAS Library Cataloguing-in-Publication Data

Wang, Gungwu, 1930–
    Wang Gungwu : *Junzi*: Scholar-Gentleman in conversation with Asad-ul Iqbal Latif.
1.   Wang, Gungwu, 1930–
2.   Scholars—Australia—Biography.
3.   Historians—Australia—Biography.
I.   Latif, Asad-ul Iqbal.
II.   Title.
CT2808 W24A31   2010

ISBN 978-981-4311-52-6 (soft cover)
ISBN 978-981-4311-53-3 (hard cover)
ISBN 978-981-4311-54-0 (e-book PDF)

Typeset by Superskill Graphics Pte Ltd
Printed in Singapore by Utopia Press Pte Ltd

Contents

Foreword

Albert Einstein once said that if his theory of relativity were proved incorrect, French people would say I am a German, and Germans would say I am a Jew. If it were proved correct, Germans would say I am a German and the French would say I am a citizen of the world. It is a tribute to Wang Gungwu as a scholar, a teacher, an administrator, and as a generous human being that every place where he has lived not only claims him but tried to attract him to stay and work there: Malaysia, England, the United States, Australia, Hong Kong, Singapore. It is also a tribute to his broad-ranging intellect that he is completely comfortable in the scholarship and cultures in the West, in China, and in Southeast Asia. It is also a tribute to the support of his wife Margaret who shares his comfort in East and West and bears his dedication to scholarship with gentle humour, understanding, and a perky optimism.

Some marginal men who span different cultures have deep psychological wounds and never feel a part of any culture. Gungwu somehow managed to sink deep roots in and feel part of many cultures, without the wounds. He had the good fortune to grow up in a gentle Chinese scholarly family as an only child speaking Mandarin and getting schooled by his schoolteacher father, especially during the Japanese occupation. Unlike his schoolmates in Ipoh, Malaya, Gungwu therefore grew up as an insider in China's "great tradition". Before and after the Japanese occupation, Gungwu also became an insider in the British school system and later in the British higher education system at the University of Malaya and the London School of Oriental and African Studies. When he studied at Central University, Nanjing in 1947–48, he had an opportunity to be a part of a group of bright young people being trained to become academic and political leaders who, as it turned out, served both in the mainland and in Taiwan.

Gungwu's teacher at the University of Malaya, C. N. Parkinson, wrote that in bureaucracies "work expands so as to fill the time available", but for Gungwu, his dedication to scholarship seemed to expand to cover all his time as he stretched from economics and Western literature to Southeast Asian history and two thousand years of Chinese history. But the political problems Malaya faced in his formative young adult years seemed to give an urgency and passion to his scholarship as he began his life-long pursuit of the big questions: how do civilizations fall apart and recreate order from chaos and how do people's identities change as they adapt to changing circumstances? At the School of Oriental and African Studies in London, he studied Chinese and Southeast Asian history and completed his Ph.D. in three years, with a thesis on the Five Dynasties that helped him better understand how a great empire (the Tang) fell apart and order was recreated. The Five Dynasties thus became a baseline for understanding his more pressing question: how did China fall apart at the end of the Qing Dynasty and what does it take to re-establish order?

Those who know Gungwu have no trouble understanding why his talents were recognized at such an early age: in 1962, at the age of 32 he became Dean of the Faculty at the University of Malaya, and the following year a full professor. When John Fairbank, a Harvard historian specializing in the Qing, was trying to lay out the pattern of China's relations to neighbouring states, contrasting it to the relations of European states to their neighbours, he called on Gungwu, who broke new grounds by describing the Ming Dynasty's relations with Southeast Asia, drawing on his unique mastery of Chinese and Southeast Asian history. By 1963, when his article appeared in Fairbank's edited collection on the *Chinese World Order* and Gungwu's own book on the Five Dynasties was reprinted by the Stanford Press, he was already recognized internationally as one of the world's leading scholars of Chinese history.

Gungwu does not simplify history, nor does he beautify outstanding historical figures. He has persisted in seeking to understand history with all its complexities. Though he did not use the term, in fact he wrote about "multiple identities" before the term became fashionable, describing the complex and changing identities of Southeast Asian Chinese as they related to China, to their local regions within China, and to the country where they lived. They have neither assimilated into Chinese nationalism nor the local nationalist majority in the countries where they lived. Wang Gungwu taught, and implemented in his own life, his belief that people of diverse heritages could enrich local cultures while being loyal citizens to their nation.

After World War II, as the colonial era drew to an end, enlightened leaders of Australia, aware of the need to work with their Asian neighbours, stood at the forefront among Western nations in their effort to deepen their understanding of Asia. With a small population,

Australia concentrated resources at the Australian National University and developed a research centre for world-class scholars, exempting them from undergraduate teaching responsibilities. From 1968 to 1986, as Professor and Head of the Department of Far Eastern History and Director of the Research School of Pacific Studies, Gungwu played a major role in helping Australians enhance their understanding of China and Southeast Asia, training several generations of scholars and political leaders.

As Vice-Chancellor of the University of Hong Kong from 1986 to 1995, Gungwu led a university ending its role training colonial servants and preparing for its new role, of training graduates for life after 1997 when China resumed sovereignty over Hong Kong. He helped expand Chinese studies, but unlike the Chinese University of Hong Kong that prepared for 1997 by focusing more heavily on Chinese studies and language, Gungwu retained and built on his university's strength in the English language and Western scholarship. He helped lay the base for the period after 1997 when many of the ablest students in mainland China sought to come to Hong Kong University, even more than to Chinese University — to perfect their English and enhance their understanding of Western scholarship.

In 1997, Gungwu took over the fledgling East Asian Institute of Singapore, originally founded with the hope of providing a moral underpinning for modern government, that had begun to define a new mission of studying economic developments. Gungwu helped to develop a new mission, of bringing historical breadth to bear in understanding mainland China. Under his leadership, the Institute has grown and prospered as he attracted to his Institute bright young mainland Chinese scholars to join other scholars studying developments in contemporary mainland China. At a time when many China research centres around the world are dominated by scholars writing highly specialized studies that only fellow specialists can understand, Gungwu led the Institute in studying the big issues facing China and writing crisp clear reports that inform not only scholars but governmental and business leaders around the world.

Gungwu has lived through an extraordinary era that brought tragic wars and political turmoil but also the end of colonialism, the rise of China, and a transition from a world dominated by the West to one where Asia is playing a much larger role. He has been blessed in recent decades to have lived in a peaceful era in which the world desperately needs and can make good use of intellectual bridge builders like Gungwu who can help us deepen our understanding as China and the rest of the world endeavour to come to terms with each other.

It has been my privilege over many decades to have joined Gungwu in scholarly meetings at Harvard University, at Hong Kong University when he was Vice-Chancellor, at his East Asia Institute at the National University of Singapore, and at conferences elsewhere in the world. As someone who is not a Chinese ethnic and not a citizen of Singapore, Malaya, or Australia, I salute Gungwu on his 80th as a citizen of the world, a model scholar and university administrator, one of the world's great intellectual bridge builders.

Professor Ezra F. Vogel
Harvard University
September 2010

Wang Gungwu: Friend, Mentor and Role Model

I first met Wang Gungwu in 1957. He had just received his Ph.D. from the School of Oriental and African Studies of London University. He returned to Singapore and began his academic career as an Assistant Lecturer in the History Department of the University of Malaya, in Singapore. The University was located at the small and charming Bukit Timah Campus. The year 1957 was also the one in which, after many years of appeals to the British colonial government, the University of Malaya started a law department. I was one of the students in that pioneering class.

The total student population at the Bukit Timah Campus was small enough for us to know the students of other departments and faculties. Although the study of law was quite demanding, we still found the time to attend the classes in other departments and faculties. Through good friends studying history, such as Chu Tee Seng, I was told about a brilliant young history lecturer, Wang Gungwu. He had an extra appeal to those of us who were members of the University Socialist Club because he was the Club's founding president. We also admired his lovely young wife, Margaret.

I had studied history at Raffles Institution and found it boring. History lessons consisted of learning by heart, facts, dates and names. Wang Gungwu's lectures on history were entirely different. The facts, dates and names were not neglected, but the emphasis was on how to frame them into a coherent narrative. To challenge our young minds, he invited us to interpret that narrative from different points of view: the official versus the non-official, the winner versus the loser, the aggressor versus the victim, etc. In 1957, Wang Gungwu was a dashing young man, charismatic and eloquent.

The members of the University Socialist Club were very passionate about our quest to build a more democratic, just and equal world. We often invited the Club's former members, such as Wang Gungwu, Lim Hock Siew, Poh Soo Kai, Ong Pang Boon, James Puthucheary, and S Woodhull, to attend our meetings and debates. My recollection was that Gungwu was more focused on his intellectual pursuits than on the political activities of the time. He held progressive left-wing views, but was not an ideologue. At that time, the Socialist Club was a big tent and accommodated a diversity of views. Those I was closest to, such as Gopinath Pillai, TPB Menon, Chu Tee Seng and Tan Guan Heng, were more attracted to the moderate views of Gungwu than to the more radical views of other friends.

In 1959, we were very sad when Gungwu decided to leave Singapore and join the pioneering group which started the University of Malaya in Pantai Valley, just outside Kuala Lumpur. From across the Causeway, we followed, with admiration, the meteoric rise of Gungwu's career: Assistant Lecturer in 1957, Lecturer in 1959, Senior Lecturer in 1961 and Professor in 1963.

In 1968, we were very proud when we heard that he was appointed Professor of Far Eastern History at the

Australian National University (ANU). We were overjoyed when we learnt, in 1975, that he was the first Asian to be appointed as the Director of the Research School of Pacific Studies at ANU. In 1986, Gungwu left Canberra to succeed Dr Rayson Huang as the Vice-Chancellor of the University of Hong Kong.

I had lost contact with Gungwu for almost 20 years, the period I had spent, first, in New York and, subsequently, in Washington, DC. I had, however, continued to follow his illustrious career from afar and read some of his publications, especially those on the Chinese overseas and the re-emergence of China.

We met again in 1992, in San Francisco. I was given a most unusual assignment that year by Mr Wee Cho Yaw, the then President of the Singapore Federation of Chinese Clan Associations (SFCCA) and Mr George Yeo, the then Minister in charge of Information and the Arts (MITA). The assignment was to submit a plan to them for the establishment of the Chinese Heritage Centre (CHC), which would be housed in the historic library building at Singapore's Nanyang Technological University. Mr Wee's chief adviser, Ms Pang Cheng Lian, and I set off on a world tour to visit other heritage centres. The trip culminated in San Francisco, the venue of the inaugural Conference of the International Society for the Studies of the Chinese Overseas. Gungwu delivered the inaugural lecture.

Pang Cheng Lian and I consulted Gungwu on the plan to establish the CHC and secured his agreement to serve on its board. He also offered to introduce us to Ms Lynn Pan, the author of the excellent book, *Sons of the Yellow Emperor*. We subsequently succeeded in persuading

Ms Pan to accept our offer to be the founding Director of the CHC. Her enduring legacy is the *Encyclopedia of the Chinese Overseas*, which she ably edited.

In the period leading up to 1997, when Hong Kong would join the PRC as a Special Administrative Area, many Western pundits were pessimistic about Hong Kong's prospects, post-1997. Probably as a reaction to the Western doom and gloom prognosis, Hong Kong University organised a series of lectures about Hong Kong's future. Gungwu invited me to deliver a lecture in the series, in which I offered a relatively optimistic view from the Southeast Asian perspective. During my visit to Hong Kong University, in September 1994, I was impressed by the esteem and affection with which Gungwu and Margaret were treated by the faculty and leaders of Hong Kong.

After a hiatus of 47 years, Gungwu and Margaret returned to Singapore in 1996. Gungwu's energy seems inexhaustible and his productivity is simply awesome. Because of his leadership of the East Asian Institute (EAI), first, as Director and, subsequently, as Chairman, he has put the EAI on the world's map of leading think-tanks on modern China. Under the leadership of Gungwu, as Chairman, and Ambassador K Kesavapany, as Director, the Institute of Southeast Asian Studies (ISEAS) has regained its pre-eminence as a world-class centre of research on Southeast Asia. Gungwu is also the founding Chairman of the Board of Governors of the Lee Kuan Yew School of Public Policy. Gungwu has empowered the dynamic Dean of the School, Professor Kishore Mahbubani, and together, they have succeeded in elevating the School, in only a few short years, to the major league of the world's elite schools of public policy. In addition to these three chairmanships, Gungwu is a member of 11 other boards in Singapore and 17 overseas. He chairs the editorial board of two journals and serves on the board of many others. He continues to author or edit one outstanding book after another.

I have known Wang Gungwu for 53 years. He is one of the most brilliant men I have had the good fortune to befriend. He is not only knowledgeable but also wise. He has been honoured both by his academic peers and by governments. Yet he is totally unspoilt by fame and success. He has always been a modest and humble man. He is, by temperament, optimistic and positive. In all the years I have known him, I have never heard him utter an unkind word about any person, institution or country. Gungwu's father was a teacher and a Confucianist. If he and his wife were alive today, they would be very proud of their only child. I think his father would approve when I describe Wang Gungwu as a living example of a Confucianist "junzi", or scholar-gentleman. His devotion to his wife of 55 years, Margaret, is an inspiration for all of us to emulate.

Professor Tommy Koh
Ambassador-at-Large;
Special Adviser
Institute of Policy Studies;
and
Chairman
National Heritage Board

Junzi
Scholar-Gentleman
by
Asad-ul Iqbal Latif

These interviews with Professor Wang Gungwu seek to convey to a general audience something of the life, times and thoughts of a leading historian, Southeast Asianist, Sinologist and public intellectual. The book felicitates him on his 80th birthday.

Wang Gungwu was born on 9 October 1930 in Surabaya to Wang Fo Wen and Ting Yien. His father came from Taizhou to teach Chinese in Surabaya. In the course of the senior Wang's career, the family moved to Malaya, and the junior Wang grew up in culturally-rich Ipoh, where he attended the English-medium Anderson School. The brutality unleashed on the Chinese during the Japanese Occupation turned his world upside down. At the end of World War II, he joined the National Central University in Nanjing, where he studied foreign languages. A different kind of upheaval — the Civil War — disrupted his studies this time. At the end of 1948, he returned to Malaya at the start of the 12-year-long Emergency which called into question the future of Malaya itself. As an undergraduate at the University of Malaya, which he joined in 1949, he read English literature, history and economics. He graduated with Honours in 1953 and obtained his Master's degree in history two years later. Among his many extracurricular achievements was his role as the founder-president of the university's Socialist Club. He received his doctorate in Chinese History from the School of Oriental and African

Studies at the University of London in 1957, the same year that Malaya gained independence. His doctorate was on the Five Dynasties, but his scholarly horizons then broadened to embrace contemporary China and the Chinese in Southeast Asia, particularly in Malaya.

After his return from London, his teaching career took him from the University of Malaya, where he taught at both the Singapore and Kuala Lumpur campuses and rose to be Professor of History; to the Australian National University where, from 1968 to 1986, he was Professor and Head of the Department of Far Eastern History and Director of the Research School of Pacific Studies. From 1986 to 1995, he was Vice-Chancellor of the University of Hong Kong. He came to Singapore in 1997 as Director of the East Asian Institute. He retired from that position in 2007 to become the institute's Chairman. He holds several other chairmanships, including that of the Board of Trustees of the Institute of Southeast Asian Studies. He is University Professor at the National University of Singapore, and Emeritus Professor at the Australian National University.

The complexities of life of the Chinese living overseas, and their interaction with China, are a motif of Professor Wang's work. It must give him no small satisfaction, therefore, that those once driven from China by want, injustice and anarchy are today helping a rising China rejoin world history mostly on Chinese terms. It has been a long but fruitful walk from the terrible 1930s.

The Times

Wang Gungwu was shaped by feral times and hostile worlds. Hostile nationalisms had torn Europe apart in World

War I. The appearance of Bolshevik Russia inaugurated an alternative source of political imagination in world affairs and prefigured the Soviet Union's role as the world capital of socialist internationalism. However, the unfinished business of the war paved the way for the rise of Nazism in Germany and fascism in Italy, which clashed with the colonial democracies of Britain and France in the global contest for national supremacy. Protectionism during the Great Depression gave this contest its cutting economic edge. Imperial Japan imported the pathological nationalisms of warlike Europe and produced a rabid Asian strain. For all its anti-Western and pan-Asian rhetoric, Japan became the foremost imperial threat to Asia, the threat within. Japan had been an ally of the Western "democracies" during World War I. But as situations, possibilities and imperatives changed, it allied itself with the fascist powers in World War II.

The contending imperialisms of an old West and a new Japan all but wrecked Asia in the 1930s. The fall of Singapore to the Japanese in February 1942 marked the beginning of the end of white colonial supremacy in Asia. Since the British had been proved to be mortals, their empire could not be eternal. However, the brutality of the Japanese invasion and occupation of Malaya and Singapore revealed how much had changed — for the worse.

Soviet resilience in World War II, America's entry into it, and Japan's spectacular nuclear defeat created the foundations of a new era. The British returned to Malaya and ran into confrontation with a range of indigenous anti-imperialist forces from democratic socialists to communists. Decolonization meant the peaceful transfer of power in Malaya, but elsewhere in Southeast Asia — notably in Vietnam but also in Indonesia — it meant ejecting imperialism forcibly from a violated indigenous space. The way was clear for the emergence of new nation-states driven by different visions of anti-colonial nationalism.

Although China had never been colonized formally, it had been traumatized since the Opium Wars by forcible incorporation into an imperial sphere of commerce and conquest. The establishment of the People's Republic of China in 1949 represented the most formidable break with the imperial past in Asia, whether that past was European or Japanese. Beijing became the second world capital of socialist internationalism. Yet, problematically, the break with an intrusive foreign past entailed in time also a break with China's indigenous past that took horrendous form in Chairman Mao Zedong's Great Proletarian Cultural Revolution.

Meanwhile, the two main victors of World War II — the United States and the Soviet Union — were embroiled in the Cold War. Japan rose out of the political economy of that war, as did Taiwan. So did China eventually in the late 1970s, when Deng Xiaoping's accession to power reversed the murderous excesses of Maoism while launching China into the ideological unknown of socialism with Chinese characteristics. The Tiananmen movement of 1989 tried unsuccessfully to claim part of that uncharted territory for democracy. Hong Kong — a nation-less non-state poised transitionally between a British past and a Chinese future — provided an essential window on the larger fortunes of the mainland. The British pull-out from Hong Kong in 1997 ended the anti-imperial phase of Chinese history that had peaked with the victory against the Japanese, followed by the eviction of the Kuomintang to Taiwan and the arrival of the People's Republic of China. Taiwan's eventual re-unification remained on the mainland's existential agenda.

The end of the Cold War and the dissolution of the Soviet Union in 1991 without World War III marked the end of what Eric Hobsbawn calls the Short 20th Century that had begun with World War I in 1914.

At the onset of the 21st century, China continued to develop furiously but peacefully; Hong Kong flourished; Japan moved towards normalcy from a period of high growth; and America presided over the emergence of a multi-polar world characterised by the rise of China and the countervailing rise of India. That a period of power transition was underway was not in doubt, but the United States remained (like its dollar, the world's default currency) the hegemon of last resort, the key provided of security goods in Asia and, arguably, the primary offshore balancer in Pacific Asia. Then came 9/11 and the new wars in Afghanistan and Iraq.

Meanwhile, the destiny of the nations of Southeast Asia, separated first by colonization and then by the Cold War, converged politically for the first time in their history. The Association of Southeast Asian Nations (ASEAN), representing all the ten countries of the region and institutionalizing their collective spirit, embarked on an ambitious but confident project to integrate the regional economies. Also, because ASEAN is non-threatening and because it has not tilted towards one power (the United States, China, India or Japan) to the exclusion of the others, it has come to play an astonishingly successful role as a clearing house for security transactions among the Asian great powers. The clearing house has many rooms, but the largest are the ASEAN Plus Three process (with China, Japan and South Korea); the East Asian Summit, which widens the ambit of that process to India, Australia and New Zealand; and the ASEAN Regional Forum, perhaps the only convincing security platform in this part of the world.

The Man

Such were the events that influenced Professor Wang's thinking and teaching. This book records his response to them on hindsight, but with his keen sense of having lived through the times of which he speaks. He responded to them as a left-liberal and without cutting ideological corners. He did so because he is not a Whig historian to whom the tales of passing times must make teleological sense; history is no story of the inevitable consummation of moments converging irreversibly one day. Instead, all institutions and edifices must be built on a very Kantian sense of the crooked timbre of humanity. However, this recognition does not make Professor Wang's interventions in public affairs episodic or his work ultimately elegiac. Like the Chinese, whether in China or in Southeast Asia, of whom he writes so intimately, the Wangian dialectic is earthy, temporal, secular, tentative and provisional to a happy fault. To listen to him — as I had the privilege of doing in the course of these interviews, conducted in the first half of 2010 — is to follow the contours of a great mind as it confronts mutability in the affairs of men and yet finds continuity in the aspirations of man. Professor Wang marvels at the majestic mysteries of classical Confucianism; he mocks the pompous hollowness of emperors in a society in terminal decay; and he embraces the lover's dawn of a revolution that devours a dead past. However, he recoils in horror from a revolution that eats its children in a Great Leap Forward; and he turns away in patrician disbelief as Chinese burn books and assault scholars in a *cultural* revolution. The humanist in him surveys that receding landscape with anger, pain and dismay, but never with despair, for despair and despondency have fallen by the wayside during China's Long March from its lost to its gained centuries.

I am grateful to Dr Vineeta Sinha and Dr Alan Baumler for permission to include two interviews that they conducted with him separately for publication in journals. The interviews appear as appendices in this book, as do Professor Wang's *curriculum vitae* and a select bibliography of his voluminous writings, both compiled by him.

What emerges from these interviews is that, just as humans make history, they are free to unmake it. Indeed, as Veronica Wedgwood observes tellingly, humans stand historically between past and future precisely because their attitude to history, based on the premises and framework that allow them to understand the past, is itself impermanent. All knowledge about humans is situational, that is, dependent on time and place. The danger, then, is to avoid being enticed into what Edward Said calls communities of interpretation that define themselves by their conflictive incompatibility with one other. Professor Wang's experience of living in Australia, where he was free to further his expertise on China, confirmed his faith in the possibilities of a multi-cultural cosmopolitanism that transcended ethnocentric Western conceptions of the Otherness of China. He looks back on his years in Australia with a particular fondness.

Life cradled Professor Wang in Surabaya, sent him to school in Ipoh, led him to Singapore, took him to London, brought him back to Malaya, invited him to Australia, nudged him on to Hong Kong, and drew him back to Singapore. Greece made Homer run epic errands for all time; there are no traffic lights in the *Iliad* and the *Odyssey*. It is the same with Wang Gungwu: His Chineseness knows no bounds, but he is as universal as a child just beginning to think. Like Tennyson's Ulysses, he is a part of all that he has met.

To the family man, the world is his family, but his family is also where the world begins for him. In his 55 years of devotion to his wife, Margaret, no quarrel has marred a single day of their marriage. A superstar smile, set against the benign sagaciousness of his calming being, no doubt helped to keep the gracious nuptial peace. Filial themselves, he and his wife handed down the joy of filial piety to their children. Their grandchildren continue to enjoy their unconditional legacy of laughter, love and peace.

What a man!

INTERVIEWS WITH
PROFESSOR WANG GUNGWU

Being Chinese in Malaya

Your father came from Taizhou to teach Chinese in Malaya.
What drew him here?

My parents came from well-established families in China that had been impoverished over a generation or two. Most Chinese had been impoverished by changing political conditions, the changeover of systems of government, the civil war, the complete collapse of the economy basically from the changes that took place when an agrarian economy found itself threatened by capitalist forces. That was so in the rest of Asia as well. With the rise of the new capitalism, of new manufacturing industries arising from the Industrial Revolution of the West, many of the local industries were killed off. And certainly in rural China, what was happening from the middle of the 19th century was the steady impoverishment of people who were producing things that they couldn't sell any more. Or, they would sell them for such a low price that they couldn't survive. However, the Chinese themselves were trying to catch up, building their own industries and so on, manufacturing cheap things, and this of course had an impact on rural industry. So that period of adaptation was, I think, perilous for families everywhere in Asia.

In that sense, my parents were not exceptional. My father actually was relatively fortunate. He had a good education at home because he came from an educated family. He got to a teachers' college that merged with the university so he was both in education and had a university education. So he had a degree — but the degree wasn't worth much. In those days, you graduated and there weren't any jobs; it's becoming like that again. The family wasn't able to help him and, so, the moment he graduated, he looked for a job. That meant a school-teaching job in those days unless you were exceptionally fortunate and received a scholarship to go to the United States. So he started out as a teacher in China and was then offered a job to come out to Southeast Asia and teach at a better salary. It was a good cause as well. The cause was to educate the overseas Chinese. It was a cause that the government actually officially endorsed. It encouraged young people to go out and teach abroad.

However, there was nothing official about the actual appointment. Some schools in Malaya were looking for teachers and my father was recruited. I have just seen a document in the archives of his former university about how it happened. This was a letter from the Zhongnan Middle School in Nanjing, where my father was teaching at the time. The letter, dated 31st December 1927, referred to a request from a Chinese secondary school in Malacca for two teachers of Chinese, English, history and geography to be recruited, and asked the university for help. The contact person at the Zhongnan school was my father. My father had earlier told me that the father of a university friend was the principal of the Pei Fong High School in Malacca and that the request had come to him. Eventually, he responded by accepting an appointment himself.

Were you close to your parents?

Yes, because I was their only child. I was totally assured of their concern for me, that they cared for me, that they loved me. I had a very secure childhood. I thought it remarkable that my parents made the most of their marriage. They had never met before they married. It was all arranged through the families. It was a marriage between families, you know, nothing personal, you see. (Laughs.) And they got along very well. They cared for each other a lot and that gave me security. I think that their marriage was successful because it was an arranged marriage. They tried harder to make it work. I grew up in a family in which there was very little friction or dissension. There were just the three of us anyway; everybody else was in China. I don't remember my parents ever quarrelling, certainly not in front of me. If they had any arguments, they would just discuss things in a very civilized way. They left an impression on me of how relations ought to be conducted. The idea of a dysfunctional family never occurred to me. I saw it in other families but I never experienced it. I consider myself very fortunate.

Why did you decide to study history?

I never expected to be an historian. History was not my first love. I was more interested in literature. My father was a literary type and I grew up with a fondness for literary things. And history in school had never been very interesting. It was all about the British empire. I learnt a lot from it but it didn't inspire me because it was somebody else's history. I never identified with it. What left a very deep impression on me was that Europeans dominated Asia and that Asians had lost out over the centuries. My choice of history at university was really quite accidental. It was the fact that the English professor, whom I admired, had gone back to England. The Economics professor was not very interesting. The History professor was a lively fellow called Parkinson, of Parkinson's Law fame, so I signed up for history in my honours year. I've said this to young people before: the subject you study doesn't have to be something that you love from the day you were born. You come across it and you develop it. And the more I studied history, the more I got interested in it.

When I decided to study history, I found that I was very interested in what was happening in China, because I had been to China. There I had studied Chinese and foreign literature and also some history. But I was also always interested in questions about China because they pertained to my own past, to my parents, for example. Why did my parents leave China? Why couldn't they go back? These questions were very much a part of my life. So what I really wanted to study was modern history. I was very interested in knowing about this class of Confucian officials, Confucian-type families from which my father and my mother came, families very dedicated to a particular school of thought and which had studied very hard to keep the system going. For generations, they had studied and passed imperial examinations. Why did these people, after so many centuries of great success, fail to respond to the challenges of the 19th century? They failed completely and within the first decade of the 20th century, they were completely wiped out. That's intriguing.

The families of my father, my mother and similar people were descendents of very clever people. Why did they fail to deal with the challenges? How could they have failed so badly that, within a decade, they were completely overthrown and a whole bunch of young people came up and just took up Western ideas, whether liberalism, capitalism, socialism, communism or whatever, which seemed more attractive than what had been there? They wanted to replace Confucianism entirely. So I was puzzled. History became more interesting as I studied it.

But this is where circumstances determined what I did. It was not possible to study the modern history of China in Malaya in those days. The communists had won in China, the Emergency was on in Malaya, and no book published in China was allowed into Malaya. Anything to do with modern China was suspect; every Chinese was a potential communist, and even the Chinese themselves thought that other Chinese were communists. It is hard to imagine that atmosphere today, when there are hardly any communists left, even in China. In the 1950s, there was no way to gain access to archives in China or Taiwan. Hence, if you wanted to be an historian of modern China in Malaya, there was little original work you could do. You would have to abandon serious research altogether.

I went back to the study of ancient China since I was still interested in the subject. I thought that I would go further back and look at how China began, what made it what it was, and why it failed eventually. Even this was difficult because the university was a very new and very small university. It had a very small library which could be housed in two floors of one bungalow on the campus. The books were well-selected but they were all Western books; it was an Englishman's idea of a college library. So there were limits to what you could do. However, unlike in the past, the graduates of Chinese schools no longer could go to China to study, even if they had the money or resources. Now, in the context of decolonization and the Cold War, the British made it very clear that if you went to China to study, you would not be allowed back again. Thus, the British explored the idea of setting up a Chinese Studies department, an Indian Studies department and a Malay Studies department — an area-studies kind of thing. A small collection of classical Chinese texts was bought and became the nucleus of a Chinese library.

So I went back to ancient history as only the ancient texts were available to me. I decided that I might as well start and learn about the early part. Fortunately, because of my Chinese education from my parents and the fact that I had been to China, I had no trouble reading the texts. That's how I went on to write about the Nanhai trade between China and Southeast Asia in the first millennium. Eventually, however, I went back to Chinese history itself for my Ph.D. The Five Dynasties attracted me. I was pretty familiar with Tang history. The collapse of the Tang Dynasty reminded me that it had broken up into all those kingdoms that would fight each other. That civil war went on for nearly 100 years. That was also what we were looking at early in the 20th century, after the end of the Qing Dynasty — a civil war that divided the country and lasted not quite so long but also for about 40 years. The questions that attracted me were: What happens when a great empire collapses? How does it recover? What does it go through? As I could not study modern Chinese history, I tried to understand the 1000 years earlier when China had been in a terrible mess as well. So that's how I began.

What makes you Chinese?

I never thought about that question when I was young.
I took it for granted. My parents were Chinese, they told
me I was Chinese, taught me Chinese, we spoke Chinese
at home, and everything in my house was Chinese. The
question never arose. All Chinese in China are like that.
My parents were first-generation Chinese in Malaya, and
took it for granted that we would just go back to China
as overseas Chinese, just sojourners temporarily working
abroad, like expatriates working abroad and then going
back home one day.

*On that point, why do you object to the term, "Chinese
diaspora"?*

It is an academic objection. I'm quite clear that the word
"diaspora" in the English language has always been used
only for the Jews. And I was confirmed in this by looking
up the earlier editions of the Oxford English Dictionary,
where "diaspora" has only one meaning — the Jewish
Diaspora. There was no other meaning. And that was true
until the 20th century. But somewhere along the way in the
20th century, the Webster's dictionary in America began to
use "diaspora" to include all kinds of migrant groups who
had formed communities abroad and still had links with
their home countries. Then social scientists decided to take
this word out of its original narrow English meaning and
to apply it to everybody else.

I find this amusing. Native speakers of English know
deep inside that this word applies only to Jews; they have

never applied it to the English. I have never seen, up till now anyway, the phrase, "English diaspora". There are diasporas for the Irish, Italians, Greeks, Arabs, Persians and Indians, but not for the English. This is where my objections start. Why are we using it in this way and what are the consequences of using it this way? I think it is very misleading to apply the term to the Chinese. They don't have this ideology of going back to China like the Jews have with Israel. Not every Jew shares this ideology of eventual return, but it is very powerful one.

The other danger of using "Chinese diaspora" is to uphold what the Chinese government used to do — treat all Chinese overseas as Chinese nationals — which is something from which the Chinese of the past few decades have been trying to escape. The use of "diaspora" resuscitates the idea of the overseas Chinese as forming one single large community that is loyal to China or one that can never be loyal to other places. This is not the reality. The mythology that a Chinese is always a Chinese and can never be loyal to any country but China conveys a totally misleading impression of what Chinese communities overseas are like today.

What are your impressions of growing up in Furnivall's "plural society" of Malaya?

I lived in a mixed community in the town of Ipoh. It is in the state of Perak, which in colonial times was a protected state under what the British called indirect rule. The British Resident really ran the place. The British created a kind of civil servants' community for

Chinese, Malays, Indians, Eurasians and others who worked for the government in one way or the other. And as a result, I grew up amongst people of different ethnic origins. The common languages were Malay and English. And most of us went to Anderson School, a government school nearby where the education was in the English medium. This was something else that we had in common because it was the nearest school. We understood what it meant to work for the same government. We recognized the Sultan of Perak as the ruler. In school, because it was a government school, there were two separate ceremonies which gave us a sense of community. One was the Queen's birthday day. And then there were the Sultan's birthday and other ceremonial occasions which had to do with him. We grew up in that sort of atmosphere. There was no sense of the nation-state. It was imperium on one side and the monarchy on the other. But neither side emphasised our ethnic origin or nationality.

The British, for all their ideas about race in their administrative calculations, didn't impose these ideas on us in any way because there were so few of them anyway. It was like India, where a few Englishmen ran a whole big district. They really depended on the locals. And as far as they were concerned, they treated the locals in the same way. Anybody who worked for the government was treated in the same way. Englishmen got special privileges, of course, but the rest were more or less the same. So, in a funny way, they created a kind of equality among the non-whites, the non-British, whether we were of Indian, Malay or Chinese origin.

Where was it?

In a place called Green Town, where the government
built a lot of housing units for civil servants who were
Malay, Chinese, Indian, Ceylonese, and so on. Most of
the Chinese were, in fact, local-born Chinese who were
English-educated because that enabled them to join the
civil service. My father was an exception. He had studied
English in his university but he came from China. Most
of the others were local Chinese from Penang and Taiping
whose families had been in Malaya over many generations
and who didn't speak much Chinese at all. Many of them
spoke English at home. And if they spoke Chinese, they
spoke only dialect, whereas for me, because we came from
China, we spoke the Chinese, Mandarin, that my parents
had brought with them from China. So that was already
exceptional. But, because I also spoke English, I was
never treated any differently from the others. We played
together, we grew up together. What changed everything
was World War II.

*How did the Japanese Occupation affect your sense of
being Chinese and Malayan?*

Well, first of all, the war was obviously a frightening
experience for everyone. For one thing, the schools
were changed. All the English schools, especially the
government schools, were turned into Japanese schools.
They didn't actually say so, but the medium of instruction
was changed to Japanese. All of us had to learn Japanese.
So my father decided that I would not go back to my

school. In any case, the community was dispersed because my father and many others did not join the Japanese civil service. He tried to find other work. So we moved away from that community and I lived in the town itself, which was mostly Chinese with some Malays and Indians. Then, because I didn't go back to my old school, my father put me for a short while in a Chinese primary school. But he pulled me out when even that school introduced more and more teaching in Japanese. In a way, I regained a sense of Chineseness when living in the Chinese town, learning Chinese from my father. There was no more English.

When the Japanese came and drove out the British, the most striking thing immediately was that the Japanese treated people differently. They distrusted the Chinese because the Chinese had resisted their conquest of China and had been running anti-Japanese campaigns. So they were very suspicious of the Chinese, and watched them very carefully. They treated the Malays differently because they were trying to woo them by saying that they were indigenous and Malaya was their country. And they pretended that they were there to save the Malays from the British, from the Chinese, from the Indians, from everybody else. That was the line that they put out to the Malays. Some Malays didn't buy that line, but there were others who were very happy to go along with it. The Japanese encouraged Malay nationalism as opposed to the others. And they encouraged Indian nationalism for Indians to join the Japanese in fighting the British and liberate India. The Japanese thus treated each group very differently.

The Japanese Occupation lasted only three-and-a-half years. It wasn't very long but it was just long enough, I think, to leave consequences behind because when the Japanese left, and when the British came back, it was never quite the same again. Prior to that, the only nationalism was somewhere else and somebody else's. You had British nationalism, Chinese nationalism, maybe some Japanese nationalism, and the Indians had their Congress. Some Malays looked to Indonesia for Melayu Raya, the Malay world, but their nationalism was not as intense as in Indonesia. They were not well organized because there were different states and the loyalty to each Sultan stood in the way of a larger nationalism. But, the war made the Malays more nationalistic partly because they were encouraged by the Japanese and partly because many of the young Malay elites had worked with the Indonesian elites whom the Japanese had brought together during their rule.

What were the consequences?

The Japanese attempt to liberate the region from the white man stimulated a variety of nationalisms. And so, it could never be the same again when the British came back: They had shown that they could be defeated and thus lost their old authority. When they came back, they had the ability to run the place because they still had the military power to do so, and the wealth in Malaya was sufficient to finance their continued rule, whereas locally, nobody was organized to do that anyway. The British tried to encourage a kind of oneness, but I think the plot was lost. They just couldn't restore it.

During the Japanese Occupation the Chinese guerillas in Force 136 had been armed by the British to fight the Japanese. Many were members of the Malayan Communist Party who fought in the jungles with British guns as allies of the British. After the war, Malay leaders were seen as having collaborated with the Japanese, and the Chinese were seen as having been on the side of the British. And now the British were victorious, the Chinese were victorious, and the Japanese were defeated. So you can imagine the tensions. It was pretty bad in the first few years.

Then the British came down to the view that the Chinese actually were likely to go with communism in China, were not trustworthy or reliable, and hence the British needed to fight on the side of the Malays against the Chinese. So the British policy of a Malayan Union was changed to that of the Federation of Malaya, to re-establish the special position of the Malays and encourage them to build up a new nation-state. They were very dramatic years, but I missed some of the drama because I finished school and went to China to study. But even in school, we were faced with this ultimate question: what would happen when the British left?

Since it was an English school, we still had the feeling that we would all go to the same schools, learn the same things together, and develop a sense of sharing and understanding which would be the basis for the new nation. But, then, I didn't really fit in because, by that time, my father had turned me into a person who was much more conscious of being Chinese and wanted to learn about things Chinese. So I went to China to study. However, no thanks to the communists in China, I had to return to Malaya. I had to rethink my whole place in the world because I found that I could not see myself as belonging to China anymore. Home was Malaya, where I had grown up with people from many races. My return shaped my sense of multi-ethnicity. I was comfortable with that.

But that changed, did it not? Why?

By that time, decolonization was on and the British were on their way out. A generation of English-educated people tried in a way to replicate a kind of post-colonial society based on principles of freedom, democracy, equality and justice. But the reality was that communalism was much deeper because it had roots. The English-educated shared those ideals, whereas the Malay-educated would look to the Malays, the Chinese-educated to the Chinese, and the Tamil-educated to the Tamils. The British wanted to encourage oneness as the basis of a new Malayan nation, but the reality was quite different.

   Then there were ideological divides encouraged by the Cold War. The communists or the left-wing were winning in China, Vietnam, Indonesia, and even in India. Others looked to the West for modernization along different principles, some capitalist, some not capitalist, just moderate, not prepared to use violence. The big break in the left occurred between those who were prepared to use violence and those who were not. People like Nehru were left-wing but they were against violence. And we were inspired also by the left wing in Europe. It was a very European, British-Labour-Party type of thing. All these nationalist leaders were more or less left-wing but they were divided between those who wanted something more constitutional and based upon the law, agreement, democracy, debate, freedom of association and so on, whereas the others wanted the use of violence.

The war in Malaya was fought out mainly in the jungles. Although it wasn't as fierce as in Indonesia or Vietnam or Burma, it was extremely nasty. Thousands of people were killed in the course of the Malayan Emergency. So the whole of Malaya was, in a way, in a state of uncertainty and I think that all of us shared that uncertainty. Most of those who had studied in English schools belonged to the group that believed in non-violent, liberal socialism — a kind of right-wing socialism, whereas those who were educated in the Malay schools tended to look to Indonesian nationalism and those who went to Chinese schools to Chinese nationalism.

Malaysia, Singapore and Australia

How did you respond to Singapore's Merger with Malaya, Sabah and Sarawak to form Malaysia?

On my return from China, I went to the University of Malaya in 1949, went on to study at the University of London, and came back to teach at the University of Malaya. I returned from London in 1957, the year the Federation of Malaya became independent. I saw that as a great beginning and decided to identify with the Federation. Of course, Singapore was out of it because it was still a British colony. The University of Malaya was actually in Singapore. But because Malaya was independent, the Malayan government, quite reasonably, said that the University of Malaya should really be in Kuala Lumpur and not in Singapore. There were big discussions about that and then they came to a compromise, which was that there would still be one University of Malaya with a division in Singapore and a division in Kuala Lumpur. In 1959, people were asked to decide which division they wanted to work in. For me, it was very obvious: I came from Malaya and so I asked to go to Kuala Lumpur. That was a clear indication that my real identity lay in the new country that was being established. And the idea of building a new university for that country to help to shape that nation was something very attractive to me. I certainly believed that that was something that I wanted to do. So I offered to go to KL.

The question of Singapore's future was left vague. Only in 1960–61 did this idea of Merger come up, with the Prime Minister of Malaya agreeing to the British proposal, but with great reservations, because the Malay leadership in Kuala Lumpur was always concerned about adding so many Chinese from Singapore to the population and changing the demographic pattern too much. So the new plan brought in Sabah and Sarawak. Of course, we were aware that demography was the real reason for the creation of Malaysia. Singapore, too, was aware of this. In order to get in, to be allowed to join Malaya, they had to persuade Sabah and Sarawak to join in too. So Singapore played a big role in getting the Sabah and Sarawak people to join Malaysia. In any case, we in Kuala Lumpur saw this as a tremendous step forward. The larger country — the Federation of Malaysia — would be really meaningful with Singapore as a part of it.

In fact, it was in that context that I led my colleagues in the university there to produce a volume called *Malaysia: A Survey*. It took us about two years. We produced it after the Merger had succeeded. Its publication was delayed somewhat by the fact that Brunei changed its mind about joining. But anyway, it was delayed long enough for it to appear only in 1964, months before Singapore was kicked out. The book was out of date within months. The Separation of Singapore was a great blow to us. There is no question about that.

Who and what were fundamentally responsible for Singapore's Separation from Malaysia?

This is something that I have to leave to historians of the future. What was clear in the lead-up to Merger was that the Malayan leaders did not really trust Singapore and were rather fearful of the whole exercise. But the Tunku was confident that it could be done, although he imposed a lot of conditions. It was also quite clear that Singapore was extremely uncomfortable and that the Singapore leaders would have tremendous trouble persuading the people of Singapore to accept Malaysia. So they, too, had to fight for very tough terms to protect Singapore's autonomy. The negotiations made it quite clear that neither side was really happy with what had been settled. But it was the best they could do. There were a lot of residual matters that could not have satisfied either side. So from the point of the negotiations, one cannot say who was responsible for the ultimate failure of the whole thing. Both sides were willing to give in to some extent, however reluctantly.

But it was also clear that tensions were actually growing between the two sides. I suppose what really happened was that because of the lack of trust, the question of political participation in the elections in Singapore and then in the elections in Malaysia was never resolved satisfactorily, so that each side accused the other of breaking the agreement when the other stood for elections in its territory. For Malays, the fact that the People's Action Party stood for Malaysian elections breached the formula on which the Malayan government was based, which was a partnership between the United Malays National Organization, the Malayan Chinese Association and the Malaysian Indian Congress. In that triangular partnership, the PAP was seen as coming in, an interloper, trying to depose the MCA and trying to replace it. That is how it was played up in Kuala Lumpur. So there were divisions within the Chinese community. Many Chinese sided with the PAP against the MCA on the grounds that the MCA was not strong enough in the negotiations and that Singapore's coming in would make a big difference.

The communal calculations were very unhealthy. Every election or political activity got to be talked of in communal terms. Singapore was theoretically standing for the opposite, for a non-communal political party. It did not fit in at all. The campaigning for the elections added to the realization on both sides that something had made a successful merger impossible. I do not know exactly when it occurred to the leaders that the only way ahead was to separate, but there were rumours at that time that extremist groups in the Malay parties were going to take extreme actions against the PAP. The Tunku was concerned that if they did something, it would lead to the complete breakdown of the country. The racial divide would be exacerbated and it would be very hard to pull back from it. It was left to the Tunku to decide what to do.

Incidentally, I was away during those critical months. I was on a fellowship at the Australian National University. I came back the day when Separation was announced. I was taken totally by surprise because none of us in Canberra expected that. The Australian High Commissioner in Kuala Lumpur, which was supposed to be very close to the Tunku and other leaders, was not aware of Separation. I know this because, the night before that, I was at a dinner party with the Australian diplomats in charge of the Malaysia Desk, and they were not aware of it. And the next day, I was lunching with a few of the same fellows. In the middle of the lunch, they were called away because the news was announced. I was absolutely shocked. So you can see how, in spite of all these tensions, we were all still vaguely hopeful that somehow, as in the past, some compromise would be found at the last minute. But it became absolutely hopeless.

However, what is important is that Separation was obviously well worked out between the leaders of Singapore and Malaysia so that, when it did occur, steps were taken to ensure that everything was peaceful, and mutual respect was proclaimed, at least publicly. Singapore was accepted as an independent nation-state and was given support in the United Nations. That was remarkable considering the underlying tensions. In the end, I think, the Malaysian government did the right thing. The Singapore government was protected in a way by the British and the Australians and the Five Power Defence Agreement. The Malaysian government gave its support, and the Singapore government did all the right things to ensure that, within a few days of the announcement, the world would accept the fact that Singapore had become a new country. To me, that was remarkable.

Do you foresee Re-Merger one day?

For months afterwards in Kuala Lumpur, there was talk that this was a temporary measure, to ease all the tensions and then, eventually, both sides would have to acknowledge that they needed each other and that, somehow or the other, they would be able to rearrange the whole thing and come back together again. The unkind view was that Singapore could not possibly survive without Malaysia, and the other aside was that the Chinese in Singapore would never accept the principles on which the Malayan government was based. It took a year before it became quite clear that Re-Merger, at least at that time, was not on the cards. And at each step of the way, everything was separated. From the newspapers to the railways and the airlines, everything was worked out like complicated divorce proceedings. And at each step of the way, it became less and less likely that Re-Merger was possible. Of course, since then, every now and then, it pops up as a question. But it's been a long time now and I think that it is most unlikely. It seems to me now that the situation is quite clear. The two governments really stand for two very different sets of principle and neither side would be prepared to compromise on that.

The Wang Gungwu Curriculum Review Committee's Report had the objective of putting Nanyang University at least on par with the University of Malaya and the University of Singapore. Ironically, many defenders of Nantah are very critical of the report. Interestingly, the committee was appointed in 1964, when Singapore was a part of Malaysia. The report was submitted to the authorities in May 1965. Singapore separated from Malaysia in August that year. The report was released in December 1965. Did the drama of the times conspire to create hostility towards the report among the Chinese-educated?

The politics of that time was actually very tense. It started to become tense, I would say, from about 1960, when the idea of Malaysia came in. The people of Singapore were already divided. Had the PAP been united at that time, it probably wouldn't have been that serious. But just prior to that, the PAP itself began to diverge on all sorts of issues, including issues about security. The Malaysia issue heightened that point even more because of those who held views different from the mainstream PAP. They disagreed with the leadership of the PAP, and saw the entry into Malaysia as dangerous because the Malaysians, backed by the British, would be willing to use the Internal Security Act against them if given a chance to do so. The internal

debates within Singapore about the Malaysia issue were
really very, very serious.

I was in Kuala Lumpur from 1959 so I can't say that
I was fully aware of all the nuances, but from what I read
and heard, I certainly recognized that this was a serious
division in the community. But for various reasons, the
PAP leaders held to the belief that merger was inevitable.
Joining Malaysia simply had to happen. And at that
time, I must confess, I agreed with that view. I thought
the idea of a totally independent Singapore didn't make
much sense. As I said to you earlier, I was sufficiently
moved by the idea of Malaysia to get people together
to write *Malaysia: A Survey*, which we published. So
I belonged to that group that thought that this was a step
in the right direction.

When I was approached to chair the Committee of
Enquiry by the Ministry of Education in Singapore, my
old friend, Ong Pang Boon, explained that the future of
Nanyang University had to be examined in the context of
Singapore becoming a part of Malaysia. I agreed. There
had been committees before whose reports I had read. He
put together the committee. I had no say in setting up the
committee. I was the only member from Malaysia. The
rest were all in Singapore, and so I would fly down for
meetings. We spent several months interviewing a lot of
people — students, the representatives of students, staff and
so on. And the purpose, as I understood it, was to look at
the curriculum in the context of Malaysia. Our objective
was to get Malaysia to acknowledge Nantah as one of
the universities of the country, give it full recognition,
recognize its degrees, and enable it to achieve the kind of

promise that it had. The key point in my mind was that the university should be treated as an institution that was equal to the other two and its graduates given the same opportunity to compete for the best jobs in the country. The students had come from the best Chinese schools in the country and were comparable to the best from the English schools. What was needed was the opportunity for them to master English and to arrange for common courses so that students from other educational streams could come and study with them and also acquire knowledge of Chinese and things Chinese. In this way, all Nantah graduates could play their part in the new country's development and the university could be an important factor in the creation of a multicultural Malaysia.

After the report was submitted, I went away to Australia. I came back to Malaysia on the day of Separation. When I passed through Singapore, I was struck by how half the people of Singapore were celebrating the exit from Malaysia. Firecrackers being let off in Kallang Airport reminded me that that a lot of people in Singapore were delighted that they had been kicked out. The night before in Sydney, I saw Lee Kuan Yew cry on television. So I was made fully aware how serious the divisions were.

I thought that the report was no longer valid because the situation had changed. The report had been submitted in May. When we came back in August, nothing had happened because everybody had been too busy fighting over this whole Separation issue. Then, suddenly, it was announced that the report had been accepted by the government of independent Singapore. People think of it as my report. It's not my report. I was Chairman of a committee. Of course, I was responsible as Chairman, but it was the report of all of us in the committee set up to get Nantah recognised as a university in Malaysia.

Some commentators blame the report for hastening Nantah's mutation from a people's seat of Chinese learning to a British-style factory of manpower planning. Is this criticism unfair?

That is not fair. The report wanted to see the University treated as a public university supported by the government, with its degrees recognised and its graduates accepted together with those of the other two. It would then be enabled to play an equal role in the development of the new Malaysian federation. What happened in Singapore after it became independent is a different story altogether. The education policy of the Singapore government after 1965 was geared to the new country's survival as a small independent country. That was a major challenge that had nothing to do with either my report or with Nantah for that matter. Frankly, I was surprised that the government pursued the report in the new context. But did it follow the report in treating Nantah as equal to the University of Singapore? I was not able to follow the politics of Singapore educational policy closely enough to know how much of the report was actually implemented. By that time, I was caught up in KL with the policy changes of the government there and did not think that the report concerned us in Malaysia. From afar, it seemed to me that what was in the report was not carried out. Independent Singapore needed a different kind of start and, as it turned out, the nature and survival of Singapore itself became a subject of bitter controversy.

What role did trilingualism in Chinese, Malay and English play in the committee's objective of rescuing Nantah and its students from intellectual and economic discrimination?

In the context of Malaysia, it seemed inevitable to us that everybody would have to learn the national language. Also, it was taken for granted that all the students would have studied Chinese already and the standard of Chinese at the time was high. The question was what should be their English requirements. It was quite clear that if you really wanted to get on in higher education and in the international world of higher education, English was not a colonial language any more. It would be different if you were in the Netherlands East Indies; then Dutch would be a colonial language, definitely a colonial language because there would be no other use for Dutch there. But English was different. English had become the language of international education. So, somehow, students would have to learn that as well. So we started with the principle that you have to know the national language and that you have to learn English. But the Chinese was taken for granted. Since 12 years of Chinese education were a given, the challenge was to pick up more Malay and English at Nantah. Then we could say to the government that our students knew Malay. They had learned the national language to show allegiance to the new country because the bulk of the students in Nantah actually came from Malaysia. Learning English would show that they could cope in the international world to help the country develop economically. Probably we were a little naive in our assumption that mastering an extra language at university would be easy. We were optimistic because we had seen individuals who had done that, but it was very difficult for most people. My later experiences have shown me that this was so. However, at the time we took the view that it was realistic and that it was something that was good for the university. We might not be able to achieve trilingualism immediately but we foresaw that soon, everybody would have studied Malay in school because that was going to be the national language. Students would have studied English, too, in school but perhaps the standard will be lower. So we set up a language centre for the university. It is in that context that Nantah was meant to be trilingual. If you look at the Malaysian students of Chinese origin today, I would say that most of those from the Chinese schools arrive at university with a reasonable command of English, Malay and Chinese and are effectively trilingual. The best of them are awesome.

To turn to a broader issue, you have spoken of "A", "B", and "C" Chinese in Malaya. How far have those categories evolved today?

When I tried to classify the different groups of Chinese, it was in the context of nation building and the choices the Chinese had to make about staying or leaving, and how to identify with their local conditions. And, as I understood it at that time, it was quite clear that those who were several generations born and brought up in the country, those who were English-educated and had grown up with Malay schoolmates, had gone to the same schools and shared a lot of the educational background together could become the core of a new nation. There were still a lot of Chinese who felt that way and they are what I call the Group C Chinese, who were prepared to commit themselves and work hard for the creation of a new nation-state called Malaysia.

And at the other extreme were the mostly first-generation Chinese or recent migrants who had arrived from China a few decades earlier and who felt tremendous enthusiasm at the new China arising out of the Chinese Communist Party's victory in Beijing. Even if the majority of these Chinese were not communist, they identified themselves with the new China and felt that they should go back there or somehow retain their Chinese nationality while working in Malaysia. I call them Group A. They would not give way on anything pertaining to Chinese interests and they thought that they could actually play a part in building on the relationship between China and Malaysia. Identification with China was central to their concerns.

But what really struck me was that, actually, the vast majority of Chinese were in between these two groups. I would not say that they were non-political. Most people say that the Chinese are non-political so long as you give them a chance to do business and make money. I was not convinced that that was the case. I was much more convinced that they were very interested in politics but kept a low profile. They were alert to what was happening but they did not believe in political commitment as such as being all that important to them. They placed importance on their families, their social connections, their business connections, and their livelihoods. They thought that if they could maintain their own culture, and were left alone basically to preserve their ethnic identity and the symbols, rituals and customs associated with it, they could accept living in Malaya and be citizens of that country. They would not play a very active part in shaping that country; at least, they were not aware of what they could do because they were so concerned with protecting their identity as Chinese. But they were definitely not prepared to associate with the country called China. They were perfectly willing to become Malayans and accept citizenship, but as Chinese inside that country. I found that this group was probably much larger than either of the A and C groups. I could not break it down any further because it was a very mixed group. And as I explored it, I thought the only way was to identify it by its unwillingness to commit itself to either the A or C Groups. I called it Group B.

I have been questioned about how I identified the people in such a group. I tried very hard but it's not possible to pin down the exact particulars that identified them. Each of them would have their own reasons for why they felt the way they did. But what they would agree on was that being Chinese in Malaya was significant and it was something that they were dedicated to protecting: their Chineseness in Malaya. But they had no loyalties to China, no intention of going back there, and no desire to work towards a kind of an amalgamation where they became

Malay individuals who no longer thought of themselves as Chinese. These were the vast majority of Chinese.

What is different now?

The situation is much, much more complicated now. The Group C, for example, now include some very discontented young people who are disillusioned by their failure to be accepted as equals by Malay leaders. Group A has shrunk. There are still some but they find any kind of identification with China or Taiwan less and less meaningful. So, in a way, Group B has grown, having been joined by some Group A Chinese who no longer look to China and perhaps also by some rather disillusioned Group C people. This latter group may also have grown because so many younger Chinese have studied in Chinese primary schools instead of the previously available English schools. But such a Group B consists of some very unhappy mix of people. They feel that they are discriminated against and that they have to work harder to protect their interests. Fewer of them are committed to the idea of a Malaysian nation than before. Earlier, they were more open to the idea. Now, they are just defensive about how they can preserve their Chineseness in the face of growing intolerance of their identity among Malays and the feeling that they have to actually work harder and be more united in order to protect it. So Groups C and B have crisscrossed a little bit. There were many in Group C who now are much more sympathetic towards the sentiments of Group B. Also, Group B feels that they can't just leave things to circumstances but needs to take

political action. So that part of it, I think, is very different
from in the past. These Chinese are much more active
politically than they were in the past. They are fighting
for a balance that could protect them from the idea of
Malay supremacy. This Groups B is unique to Malaysia,
I think. It is the group that is worth close attention, both
its composition and its size.

*Will multiracialism hold in Malaysia, or will it be replaced
by multiple racisms?*

That's putting it very nicely. I think multiculturalism
was the ideal. It has not been abandoned as an ideal.
However, the number of people who believe in it as
something feasible may actually have gone down compared
to the past. But I think there are no accurate estimates
of those people. We do not, for example, feel confident
that people would tell you exactly what they think today.
I meet lots of Malaysians of Chinese or Indian or Malay
descent, and when I ask them, they say that they hope
for multiracialism. But if you pursue things deeper and
then ask them other questions, you will realize that this
is some vague distant thing but, in practice, what they
are really concerned about, on a day-to-day basis, is how
communalism is getting worse and how there is a lack
of communication between the communities. The lack of
trust is growing. People don't tell each other the truth any
more. They don't even want to associate with each other;
they don't eat together, and they don't invite each other
home. That's becoming the norm. People are moving away
from that ideal. And it is fading.

You have talked about Malaysia. How does Singapore compare with it?

Singapore, I think, took a different line. Rightly or wrongly, it took the line that integrating the community is not something that can be done quickly. In the meantime, communities needed to be treated as being separate, but sensitivity and mutual respect had to be developed consciously. The reasons are fairly simple. Unlike Malaysia, Indonesia and other places where there are people who claim that they are indigenous, Singapore cannot claim that. Nobody can really talk about indigenousness here. The descendants of those who can claim to have been here in 1819 are so small that the number doesn't matter. So, in a way, Singapore is a kind of migrant society and state, rather like America and Australia. It consists of migrants. And then the question of who came first is of no consequence after a while because they were all migrants. You recognize that integration is the basis of your stay.

I think that this is where Singapore is a complete outsider in this region because it is the only one that recognizes that it is a migrant state. Other states have many migrants but this one is a migrant state. Therefore, the model of United States, the Americas and Australasia is closer to Singapore than are the models of Europe. Indigenous states look to the European model as the basis of nation-state building. To this day, you can see the Europeans struggling with that. They don't like migrants and are always arguing about less immigration because the argument is that they are an indigenous state, a native state and immigrants bring in strange habits and customs which upset the "native" people.

Singapore stands out as being totally different. It follows what the migrant states are doing and then recognizes the rights of everybody as equal. The majority came from China and had to earn their rights by being loyal to the new state. That takes time. And Singapore has made sure that the minorities don't feel that this is going to be a Chinese state. In order to do that, the leadership had to go out of its way to underline this migrant nature of Singapore, that everybody is equally a migrant, that everybody has the right and the opportunity to help to build up the state, that nobody has any priority, and that nobody should be discriminated against. You've decided to make your home here, you've made your commitment, and that is the basis on which you are a Singaporean.

What drew you to Australia?

For twelve academic years after returning from London in 1957, I taught at the University of Malaya in Kuala Lumpur and Singapore. Too much of my time was taken up by teaching, and later by administrative work as Professor and Head of the Department of History. Also, I was keenly interested in the role of a university in the life of a young nation. As an historian, I was fascinated with the question of how to build a nation out of such a mix of different people. Malaya was obviously not a nation. When the Dutch or the Americans became independent, they were basically one people, whereas we had different nationalisms — Chinese, Indian and Malay. Malay nationalism itself was diverse, ranging from an aristocratic loyalty to the Sultanate, to loyalty to the Malay race as a whole, to a larger loyalty to Islam. I was inspired by the universities of the West, where there was a tradition of freedom that encouraged academics to think and do the kind of work that would help the human condition. I thought that our new nations needed good universities. So I got drawn into social and semi-political activities that had to do with nation-building, with students and staff, and with how academic disciplines and courses were organized, mainly in the Faculty of Arts.

I enjoyed doing all this because I loved my students, but I was getting too involved. I realized that I was not doing enough research. I received offers from abroad. I wasn't interested in Britain or America, but the Australian offer interested me, partly because I liked the country and partly because it was a research job with no undergraduate teaching and few administrative duties. I consulted my wife, and she supported me. I wasn't thinking of going away for a long time, perhaps only for three to five years. The University of Malaya agreed, but it couldn't accept my request that an additional professor to me be appointed. In those days, the university did not have two Chairs in the same department, and if there were not, I would not have a Chair to return to. But if another professor were not appointed, I was afraid that a department without a professorial head would find it difficult to develop. I did not want to leave our young department in such a vulnerable position. In any case, although having a second Chair would not have cost the university anything for several years since I would be away on no-pay leave, my suggestion was turned down. So I resigned and went off to Australia.

Being at the Australian National University (ANU) was a fantastic experience. The university had an excellent library, and as did the National Library, located a few miles away, which was modelled on the Library of Congress. The two libraries cooperated so that they did not duplicate their books. They bought a lot of good books on China. This was one of the reasons that I turned to the study of China again. At the University of Malaya, I had concentrated on Malayan and Southeast Asian history, but the Cultural Revolution refocused my attention on China. I wanted to know how young Chinese could do such violence to their own history and culture by destroying temples and burning books. Unlike the anti-communist world in Malaya in which I had lived, where books on contemporary China were banned, Australia was a wonderful place to gain access to resources on the Cultural Revolution in English, in Chinese, and in translation. I just fell in love with the conditions in which scholars worked and stayed on in Australia for 18 years.

The ANU gave me tenure straight away as a research professor at the Research School of Pacific Studies. I supervised only doctoral students; there was no undergraduate teaching. It was an excellent university. The Australians were very good to me. Australia at the time was associated with the White Australia policy, but it had begun to change. Young Australian intellectuals were ashamed of that policy, which they considered wrong. It was a foolish policy even from the point of view of the national interest because Australia needed Asians. So the educated classes went about trying to trying to get the politicians to change the policy. Smart politicians, top bureaucrats and academics knew about the importance of Asia. In fact, there were many enlightened Australian journalists who had worked in China or Japan and knew Asia first-hand. So, if you add up the total awareness of Asia, I would say that Australia led the white man's world. Even the percentage of Americans who were aware of Asia then was miniscule, and the Europeans did not care very much. Educated Australians were fully aware that Australia had to be a part of Asia. Their problem was that Asians did not accept them because of their White Australia policy, but they struggled to be some part of Asia. I had the pleasure of seeing this group of people, including my students, grow up. [Former Australian Prime Minister] Kevid Rudd, who studied Southeast Asia and China, is an example of such people. There were also schoolteachers and trade union leaders — ironically, the key people behind the White Australia policy in previous generations — who grew close to Asia. I was part of the generation of teachers who encouraged Australian interest in Asia from the 1960s onwards.

What led you to take up Australian citizenship?

Two things were important. One was that two of my children were not born in Malaysia, and they came out with me to Australia. When I tried to register them as Malaysians, there were problems. My son had been born in London before Malayan independence. After independence we got him a passport and verified with the immigration department that he was registered as a Malayan and he travelled on that passport to Australia. When he came of age to get an identity card, my wife brought him back to Malaysia to get one but there were all kinds of problems. My wife and the boy were sent from pillar to post.

Was it racism? Which year was that?

It was December 1974.

Aha.

Whatever the reason, they were given the run around. Although he had a Malaysian passport, the immigration officials just wouldn't give him a Malaysian identity card. At the end of it all, my son was really upset. I could have taken the issue to higher levels, but the boy didn't want to be a Malaysian any more. He liked Australia. So we left it at that. As far as we were concerned, he was a Malaysian citizen with a Malaysian passport, but we got fed up with the intricacies of the legal system. He became an Australian when he turned 18. So did his two sisters. So eventually did I, and finally their mother.

That was one factor. The other factor was much more direct. Australia established relations with China at the end of 1972. In 1973, my colleague, Anthony Low, and I led a team of scholars to China. I got special permission from the Malaysian government to go as Malaysia did not allow Malaysian Chinese to go to China at that time. After that, many of my students and scholars went to China to do research. Two or three years later, I asked to go again. The first time I had asked, I had been allowed to go; the Malaysian High Commissioner in Canberra must have pulled some strings. The second time, the High Commissioner supported me again, but Kuala Lumpur turned it down. I was told later on that the Minister for Home Affairs took the view that I had been there once and wondered why I was asking to go again. I knew him: He always thought I was a bit on the left and probably suspected me of harbouring communist sympathies. So he refused. Here I was, an academic and scholar. My students and colleagues were going to China. I needed to do research. How could I pursue my profession if I didn't go to China? I asked Kuala Lumpur for permission again, and I was turned down again. So I became an Australian citizen.

How did citizenship feel on the first day?

I appreciate the openness and friendliness of Australians and their willingness to accept me from day one of my presence there, not only when I became a citizen. Mind you, I had been treated very well in Malaysia as well. A scholar and university teacher was regarded with respect in both Malaysia and Australia. What happened was that the Australians appointed me as a professor and treated me well. As for life outside Canberra, I don't know: I might have been treated very differently had I gone to a pub or something in Sydney or Melbourne. But Canberra is full of civil servants, diplomats and scholars, and hardly anyone else. I was very fortunate because, living in that environment, I never encountered racial discrimination.

So I appreciated Australia, its international, cosmopolitan atmosphere, and its genuine interest in understanding Asia. My wife and children had the same experience of living in a society that was pushing for multiculturalism. The Australians were the first in any white man's country to teach Asian languages in primary school. Australia was an open country where people could experiment and offer ideas. Australians were torn between belonging to their European roots and wanting to belong to Asia. The aspirations of most of the thinking people were very positive.

Has Australia succeeded in moving beyond being just a multiracial society to being a multicultural society?

Australian leaders — the enlightened ones anyway — certainly believe in multiculturalism. The bulk of the young Australians went through a period of genuinely supporting the ideal of multiracialism, multiculturalism and so on. And that remains the policy of the government, which has been accepting migrants from all over the world steadily. But of course, this doesn't actually change the way people live and think and there is an Australian way of life that, whether we can define it exactly or not, derives from the British way of life. And that is the bottom line and they have been like that for over 150 years with a clear 90 per cent of people coming from the British Isles in the years up to World War II. Only in the past few decades have the proportions changed. So there is a genuine feeling that there is a cultural environment which must be the basis for the Australian state. Whatever your origins — and they are quite open about that — so long as you believe in those basic values and you commit yourself to them, you will be accepted.

This is no different from America, except that America is less British. Australia is still very British. Nevertheless, Americans still have a kind of Western European civilization at their core, from their Constitution down, as it were. And provided you believe in that, then it doesn't matter what your origins are. The Australians have moved to that position, not quite as openly and ideologically as have the Americans, but they are inclined to accept it as a principle of their nation-building. Of course, there remain areas of doubt and tension over the extent to which newcomers or migrants of non-British origin can really become like that. It will take time but, ultimately, Australians would expect the vast majority of the immigrants to accept and then shape the values of Australia. The major disconnect in this argument is the place of the Aborigines. How much of their original cultures should be recognised as integral parts of the ultimate Australian culture? There is a guilt side to it, although many intellectuals have tried to resolve it. The British-origin majority are committed to the set of values that established the nation. Multiracialism is based, therefore, on some of the underlying principles they inherited.

Most of your academic life has been spent teaching in Malaya/Singapore, Hong Kong and Australia. Where — and how — have you found the greatest scholarly fulfilment?

I can't answer that question easily. My own experience has been that I have been fulfilled in my scholarly life wherever I have been able to do my work. I have complained about the fact that I couldn't work on modern China in Singapore and Malaya during the Emergency but, then, I did something else when I lived there and found the nation-building challenge most absorbing. And in every society, every university in which I've been, the environment for research and academic pursuits has been very good. In the end, scholarly fulfilment comes from within.

Now, there are some environments where the state or its officials keep on interfering, ordering you to do this and not to do that. I've been very fortunate that, all my life, nobody has told me what I could and could not do. I am lucky because I know people in countries like China, friends of mine, who have done their work in environments that have been awful. I really admire them. To have done what I have done in the environment in which I have been is not so remarkable because I worked in such favourable conditions.

Vietnam

What did the First and Second Indochina Wars mean to you in your formative years?

The end of World War II was an exciting time for all young people in Asia. At school, we were increasingly conscious that nationalist anti-colonial sentiments were growing around us and that the British were under pressure to pull back from their empire and return home. We also saw that the Dutch in their East Indies and the French in

Indochina faced the same problems. I did not pay much attention to the war in Indochina at the beginning. Apart from the tensions building up in Malaya between the British Military Administration and the various activist groups organized by the Malayan Communist Party, what was more directly relevant to us was the war for Indonesian independence, especially where it concerned the Malay states on the other side of the Malacca Straits. But we were also interested in what was happening in India and Burma where the British were clearly unable to assert the kind of control they had wielded before the Pacific War had begun. I saw the French forces, clearly weaker than the British, fighting a losing battle to do the same thing, and did not think much of the efforts they made to shore up their positions in the three states of Vietnam, Cambodia and Laos. I simply assumed that they would have to leave sooner or later, and soonest from Vietnam where the nationalist forces were strongest.

In any case, I went to China in 1947 and, for more than a year, Southeast Asia was largely out of sight and out of mind. The civil war in China dominated our lives when we were not actually studying. I can only recall two strong impressions of other parts of Asia during my year and a half in Nanjing. The first was the independence of India followed by the assassination of Gandhi, on which subject the Chinese newspapers reported in great detail. The other was the Emergency Declaration in Malaya that my parents wrote to me about, not least the dangers that my father faced each time he visited Chinese schools in the towns and villages of the state of Perak, where many Chinese who were living outside the main towns were being killed. The Indochina War, in comparison, did not register at all.

It was not until 1949 after I had returned to Ipoh that I realized how much anti-colonialism had made progress in the region. Again, the communist victory in China cast a much larger shadow than anything else. The effect of that on communist parties in nearby countries was clear. However, by that time, I had learnt enough of Chinese history to know that the Vietnamese had no love of China in its imperial past. That was how I understood the willingness of various Vietnamese leaders to look to the French, the Americans and the internationalist communist movement, for arrangements that could ensure their country's ultimate independence. My stay in Nanjing in 1947–1948 had alerted me to the tremendous problems that the new regime in Beijing faced to bring order to the country, and I did not see China playing any significant role in the Vietnam War. The events leading to the Vietnamese defeat of the French armies at Dien Bien Phu thus did not surprise me. It was a victory led by dedicated patriots who produced results that strengthened their bargaining position at the Geneva Conference being held at that time. This encouraged them to believe that a united and independent Vietnam was within sight.

My interest in the Second Indochina War was thus largely focused on Vietnam. I understood that neither Cambodia nor Laos could be independent players. Instead, I thought that the elections agreed on at Geneva would lead to Vietnam's reunification under the leadership of Ho Chi Minh and separate nationhood for each of the other two territories. Ho Chi Minh was one of my anti-colonial heroes at the time. I was, therefore, frankly surprised that the Americans who had been so sympathetic to other independence movements earlier on would take over from the French and try to determine Vietnam's future.

In 1965, I wrote an essay, "The Vietnam Issue", about why American intervention in that war was unjustified. I realised that the decision to do so might have had something to do with their relative success in Korea. It was influenced by the fact that the international efforts in Korea had been successful in holding the line against communism. In the case of South Korea, North Korea attacked it, and the United States, with the backing of the United Nations, intervened with massive force and helped to stop the North Koreans and, eventually, in spite of the Chinese intervention, an armistice was signed that exists to this day. Perhaps that encouraged the Americans to believe that if they did the same in Vietnam, they could hold the line and allow South Vietnam to survive and to develop as South Korea had done. After all, the border between North and South was a narrow neck, so things should have been easier in Vietnam.

The US decision surprised me because the conditions seemed to be very different. I certainly thought that the Korean analogy was totally unjustified because the Korean War occurred after the peninsula had been divided at the end of World War II. There had been an agreement between the United States and the Soviet Union. By 1950, the newly-established People's Republic of China had a strategic interest in the peninsula and was concerned to share that with the Soviet Union. Both, therefore, wanted the total withdrawal of American troops. The Soviets also had other historical and ideological matters to be resolved following the advent of the Cold War. In any case, for them to have encouraged Kim Il Sung, they must have thought that reunification of the Koreas was entirely feasible. In that context, Kim Il Sung gambled on a swift victory and misjudged the will of the Americans to organize counter-attacks.

In the case of Vietnam, however, this was a case of decolonization in Southeast Asia. There was no question that the Vietnamese didn't want the French around anymore. The French put up a fight, and it was clear that they were losing, as they were to lose in Algeria and elsewhere. Sooner or later, they would have to go. In conditions of decolonization, why should the French be any exception? At least, the British were smart enough to see the writing on the wall and make plans to leave in an orderly manner so as to retain at least the respect of the people they were leaving. Many of us had hoped that the French, too, would see the light.

However, because the communists won in China in 1949, the Americans changed their stance and decided that they would not let Vietnam go communist. The domino theory was brought into the argument. They decided to fight in Vietnam in the Cold War framework against the communist threat to the Southeast Asia. Thus they set aside the decolonization process that they had earlier supported. They shifted from support for decolonization, which all of us appreciated, to supporting the colonial power, France.

Through all that, I remained on the side of the people who believed that Vietnam was part of a decolonization process in which the Americans had intervened for the wrong reasons. As an historian, I had read up on the history of the unhappy relationship between China and Vietnam as well as the no less complicated one that Vietnam had with its Southeast Asian neighbours. Although Vietnam had communist leaders, driving the Vietnamese to the point of turning to the Chinese for help was hardly what the Vietnamese would have appreciated. But Presidents Kennedy and Johnson saw the war as part of a larger global conflict with the Soviet bloc and the bottom line was about choosing between being either communist or freedom. I believe that this left the Vietnamese with no choice but to fight to the bitter end.

So that's how I saw it: It was decolonization being frustrated. The Vietnamese response was essentially one of nationalism. Communism was a part of it, but nationalism was much more powerful than communism. Vietnamese nationalism applied not only to the French but also to the Chinese, because the Vietnamese didn't want, as it were, to move from being a French colony to being a Chinese dependency.

The communist revolutions in China and then Vietnam were strongly internationalist in their ideological origins, but they were even more strongly nationalist in their impetus and consequences. What does revolutionary nationalism say about revolutionary internationalism?

Actually, I think internationalism never overcame nationalism even in the experience of Europe. A good example is the fate of communism in Russia compared to Germany. At the end of World War I, the supporters of Rosa Luxemburg and the German communist movement lost out to Hitler's national socialism. Once nationalism came up, this question of internationalism and the community of workers was set aside. The percentage of German workers who were sympathetic towards the Soviet Revolution was probably quite high at one point. But by the 1920s, when Germany lost the war, the question of rebuilding Germany appealed much more than did internationalism. And the campaign against internationalism took off quite easily. Of course, there was resistance by labour unions of the left in France and Italy, which tried to fight back. But you have to note that in each of these countries, the right wing, the Conservatives, the Fascists, the Nazis, in the end all won against the internationalists. Even in Europe, the home of communism, where the idea itself began, internationalism was not accepted.

That's one part. The other part is that the Chinese also soon discovered this truth in their dealings with the Soviets in the 1920s and 1930s. Mao Zedong remained very sceptical about Stalin. He was dependent on Stalin and very frightened of him, but the Chinese did understand that there was a Russian/Soviet nationalist aspect that might stand in the way of the brotherhood of all workers. They had reservations. The Chinese deeply appreciated the fact that nationalism could not be discounted because they recognized that their own communist party had succeeded largely because of nationalism in the fight against the Japanese. Had it not been for the Japanese war in China, communism might not have won. In fact, it was not clear at all that they would win in 1945. It was really a case of the Kuomintang being defeated than the communists winning. Admittedly, it was a bit of both, but the fact was that the Kuomintang was in a state of chaos and the corruption was so bad that it had no capacity to defend China in an effective way.

Nationalism was much more powerful than most of us who were socialistic in one way or the other realized. By the time of the Vietnam War, I was very sceptical that internationalism could win against nationalism. Internationalism was the means used by the nationalists to drive out the French and regain their country.

Revolutions are dramatically violent by their very nature. However, there are those who say that states are no less culpable because they are sustained ultimately by the quiet, rationalised violence of everyday life. Does violence have a permissible role in politics?

Ideally, it should not, but there is no question that states throughout history have reserved the right to use violence against those who oppose them. That has always been true, no matter who the ruler has been. It doesn't matter whether it's a monarch, an emperor, chief of the communist party, or chief of the Nazi party, or head of a democratic country. If he sees his right to rule as being legitimate and somebody opposes it, he will feel justified in using violence in the name of God, in the name of Heaven, or whatever name he chooses — some divine right that gives the ruler the moral authority to use violence against those who are opposing the right of God or Heaven. As they saw it, the legitimacy of the ruler must be protected by whatever means necessary. And that justifies their use of violence against anybody. So, I'm afraid, that is deeply rooted in every state and every kind of state.

What has happened in the past hundred years,
particularly in the Western world, is that the people have
tried, through democratic means and through certain ideals
about freedom and equality, to find ways of limiting that
right of elected governments to do certain things. But
the right has not been abolished. For example, the state
can execute people in the name of treason or some other
crime. Underlying it all, the state wants to have at least
the reserve powers to exercise that right if and when it
thinks it necessary. Declaring war is part and parcel of the
same reserve right to defend the legitimacy of sovereignty
or whatever reason you use. You can evoke the name of
God, Heaven or your Constitution. You must have the right
to defend your country by all means necessary, however
unpleasant, when necessary.

In Asia, the readiness of rulers to kill not only
their enemies but also their disobedient subjects was
something taken for granted. Confucian mandarins,
Brahmin advisers and wise Bendaharas all had the duty
to ameliorate the despotic urges of their emperors, rajas
and sultans, and there were texts and memorials to that
effect in surviving records. But none disputed the right
of the rulers to exercise violence on their peoples if they
thought their legitimacy was being challenged. However,
the opposite situation is also possible. As Mencius argued,
and later Confucians supported in principle, the people
had the right to rebel and use violence against unjust and
incompetent rulers. If and when they did that, Heaven's
will was revealed when the rebels won decisively on the
battlefield. By winning the Mandate of Heaven, the new
regime was guaranteed its moment of legitimacy: the
King is dead, long live the King! The revolution was

thus justified and complete. I saw the Vietnamese War as one fought in that tradition.

How would you have preferred the Vietnam War to have ended? You are laughing!

No, I'm not, really. I think it ended about right. The Vietnamese got their independence and that's what they are: independent. Whether they are communist or not is, in a way, irrelevant. I think that they are not particularly communist. They got their independence, set up a state, and will stand up to other states. They are exercising themselves as a state with national goals of self-protection, preservation, and so on. In that sense, it has nothing to do with the communist revolution. Communism served the purpose of enabling them to organize themselves in the most efficient way possible in the circumstances, to gain the national sovereignty that they wanted for themselves. So, it ended more or less right.

Hong Kong

You were Vice-Chancellor of the University of Hong Kong from 1986 to 1995, crucial years leading up to the British colony's return to China. Did you accept the offer to be Vice-Chancellor partly because you wanted to have a ringside view of history?

Well, I don't think I thought in terms of having a ringside view. Indeed, I never expected to be a Vice-Chancellor.

I never aspired to the job, but when the invitation came, I had to think about why I would want to go. I was not particularly attracted to the idea of being a Vice-Chancellor but I was attracted to the idea of being in Hong Kong while something so important was taking place. Coming from a former British colony, I was naturally conscious of the fact that this was the last major colony of the British but, at the same time, I was also aware that this was a very different kind of colony.

Indeed, it was customary before 1997 to refer to Hong Kong as a "territory" instead of a "colony".

Hong Kong has never been accepted as a colony by the Chinese government. The Chinese always regarded Hong Kong as a territory that was taken from them by force. At least since the revolutionary government and even before that, I think, they never thought of it as something permanent. And the idea that Hong Kong should be permanently separated from China was not acceptable to Chinese leaders. They had lost Hong Kong in war and they would like to get it back one day. Thus, how they would get it back, how the British would decolonize in this particular case, was of considerable interest to me.

The British knew, of course, that the Chinese never regarded Hong Kong as a colony. One of the reasons why the Chinese did not want Hong Kong to be considered a colony was that the decolonization committee of the United Nations took it for granted that decolonization meant the eventual independence of that colony. And so, the Chinese wanted Hong Kong to be taken out of the

UN decolonization committee. It was done in 1972 and, after that, Hong Kong was no longer called a colony. The British accepted that as the basis on which they would then continue in Hong Kong, knowing very well that there was a treaty about returning the New Territories, a large part of Hong Kong, after 99 years, which would fall in 1997. That was understood. So the question that the British had to face was: could Hong Kong and the bits of Kowloon that had been ceded, survive without the New Territories because Britain had integrated the whole place in the course of its rule there? I think the British realized that Hong Kong without the New Territories was probably not viable. It's not like Singapore without Malaya. It's quite a different kind of issue.

And the Chinese would say that it was all a matter of time. There was increasing acceptance on both sides that, when the time came, Hong Kong, Kowloon and the New Territories would be considered as one territory. What would be negotiated would be whether all of it went back to China, or whether the British could find some role for themselves in Hong Kong. I think that was the understanding when they took Hong Kong out of the decolonization committee.

And the British had no choice but to accept that, because there was no question of Hong Kong becoming independent. This was of course the central idea, because every colony that the British had left became independent. But in the case of Hong Kong, the Chinese made it very clear to them that there was no question of Hong Kong becoming independent. And that is of course one of the things about which many Hong Kong people were unhappy with the British. They were not consulted on this matter and the British had taken away their chance to argue for an independent Hong Kong. But, frankly, that was not realistic.

You were in Hong Kong when the Tiananmen Massacre of 1989 occurred. How did events in Beijing and elsewhere on mainland China affect Hong Kong residents' perception of their return to Chinese rule?

I recall that when I first arrived in Hong Kong in 1986, things looked quite good for the first few months I was there. But it was already clear that someone like Hu Yaobang, who had been chosen to be the Party Secretary by Deng Xiaoping himself, was beginning to take decisions that the old guard of the more conservative members of the Communist Party leadership were very unhappy with. They thought that he was going too far, too fast. He was liberalizing on many fronts. He was encouraging the young people to think for themselves, to some extent anyway. In Hu Yaobang's mind, it was in the interest of the Communist Party to be more progressive and open. To him, this was part and parcel of what Deng Xiaoping had in mind about economic reforms and the opening of China. So I think Hu believed that he was working in the spirit of what came from the reform decisions of 1978. But the tension building within the party about what Hu Yaobang was doing was getting very serious by the time I arrived in Hong Kong. I had the sense that something was not well, and the media reflected that unease.

However, it came as a surprise when, at the end of 1986, Hu Yaobang was removed. That was quite a major decision taken by Deng Xiaoping. The circumstances were very complicated and arose from divisions within the party. Hu Yaobang no longer represented the majority view of the top leaders in the party but was pandering too much, in their view, to the wishes of the young. Mind you, the young were very critical of Hu Yaobang because they felt that he had not gone far enough. So, in that sense, it was rather tragic that he was sacked.

When he was sacked, there was a reshuffle in which Zhao Ziyang, who was the Premier at the time, was appointed the Party Secretary, and Deng Xiaoping appointed Li Peng as Premier. I don't think that anybody was consulted. It was Deng Xiaoping himself who sorted out the new arrangements. But the sacking of Hu Yaobang actually made him a hero in the eyes of the young. Although they had been critical of him, they suddenly saw him as the most progressive person among the leadership and understood that it was his willingness to be progressive that caused him to lose his job. So they felt a sense of loss.

As far as people of Hong Kong was concerned, there were other concerns. The agreement between the British and the Chinese had been signed in 1983, and Hong Kong would be handed over to China in 14 years. So the question was of preparing themselves for that. Divisions within the Hong Kong community were becoming quite clear. Hong Kong is a complex society. There were four major groups of different sizes. One was essentially pro-British or dependent on the British to help them. Another looked to China as the future for which they had to prepare. They had to work with the Chinese, who were very helpful to those who looked to them.

The third group, a smaller yet significant one, identified with Taiwan because it was China to them, the China that had been defeated but was not communist and hence represented a perfectly good cause. They were loyal to the Kuomintang in Taiwan, which they saw as having reformed itself to a great extent. They felt that it should have a chance to offer its ideas to China. This group was vocal, with their own newspaper and representatives in Taiwan.

The fourth group consisted of an emerging group of loyal Hongkongers whose main interest was in Hong Kong. If they had a say, they would like Hong Kong to become independent. But it was quite clear that there was no way Hong Kong would be independent. So the challenge was to fight for a high degree of autonomy, a phrase that is not easy to define in terms of how much autonomy they could get out of the Chinese. They represented a growing group among young people who felt that Hong Kong's interests were very different from those of China, Taiwan and Britain.

Meanwhile, the British were beginning to introduce some democracy at the local level of the municipalities. And Hong Kong people were testing it and liking it. They were electing people who were not necessarily the people that the British would have liked. So local democracy was bringing to the fore the four groups that I have mentioned. All of them were competing for electoral places, with the native Hong Kong interest getting more and more strongly represented through the democratic process.

Let me give you an example of the Hong Kong interest. There had long been the issue of building a nuclear plant in southern China to produce electricity. The French had agreed to build it, and some Hong Kong investors were involved. When the building of the plant was announced, there was a massive movement in Hong Kong against it because it would be just across the border and would affect Hong Kong adversely if anything went wrong at the plant. This was not long after the Chernobyl accident. The people of Hong Kong were surprisingly united on a very large scale on that issue, and they marched in protest about it. I would say that this was the first major demonstration with the political intent to persuade China to change its decision, to criticise openly the people who had taken that decision.

It was very impressive. The British noticed it and the Chinese noticed it because there were half a million people out on the streets. The democratic leaders of Hong Kong emerged from this demonstration. People like Martin Lee and Szeto Wah came out of that crowd and showed their leadership qualities because of the way they had expressed the feelings of the people. I watched that with interest. Democratic forces had been unleashed to some extent by the British, slowly but significantly. Certainly, my students at Hong Kong University were deeply touched. Many of them were involved in it and many of them learned about democracy in that way.

One other thing that was very striking was that all this was occurring while the Chinese were trying to establish a kind of Constitution for Hong Kong, called the Basic Law. They tried to appease the Hong Kong people, tried to understand what they wanted, and what they were prepared to accept. And it was quite clear that the confidence of the Hong Kong people was growing that they would now finally have some say in the preparation of the Basic Law.

The Chinese, on their part, were reasonably flexible. Things were moving in the right direction.

To give you an example of how good relationships were, at Hong Kong University for example, we would have many graduate students from China. There were arrangements for them to take up scholarships with us. Ultimately, they would return to jobs in China. All this was handled with, I would say, great sensitivity by both sides and everything was going very well. The Chinese wanted their students doing graduate studies abroad to return to China and were happy that Hong Kong would not wish to keep them in Hong Kong. I was delighted and made several trips to China to increase cooperation between HKU and the university authorities in China. They made it quite clear that nothing would please them more than to have the universities in Hong Kong perform well and be well regarded.

The lesson that I took from that was that, if we were really run well, if our standards were very high for staff and students, if our research was good and if our international standing was high, the Chinese would not interfere with the universities. They would argue with the British about all sorts of other subjects but never about higher education. They were very respectful of good-quality higher education and they recognized that our universities were better than what was available in China. They knew that they had a long way to go because they were starting from a lower base and had a lot of other problems that were rooted in their own ideological problems of the past. Thus, from our point of view, everything was moving in the right direction.

So it was extremely tragic when Tiananmen occurred because, although Hong Kong people were aware of the inflation in China and the corruption in high places, the relationship was good on the whole. Then came the death of Hu Yaobang in April 1989. It triggered off the whole thing because what young people remembered was that he had been a good man whom they should have supported more. They used his death to demonstrate what they thought was important: to show respect to Hu Yaobang for having been on the right side of history and then to show their dissatisfaction by shouting slogans against corruption and inflation. They came out in large numbers. However, in the build-up to that, what had been a series of very minor demonstrations of affection and remembrance became heightened by policies the details of which are too complicated and unclear to go into here.

The climax was an editorial in *The People's Daily* that condemned the young demonstrating students as being anti-party and ill-intentioned. It really angered them. Till that point, they really weren't anti-government in any big way: They wanted to have some sign of the government responding to the problems of corruption and inflation. But now there were even more demonstrations that more people joined. It became more and more tense. Mistakes were made on both sides, frankly. The government did some really foolish things like insisting on using buildings beside Tiananmen Square for the Asian Development Bank meeting, and insisting on welcoming [Soviet leader Mikhail] Gorbachev there, with the international media brought in specially for the occasion. Until then, the international media didn't know what was really happening. But for

Gorbachev, they all came — hundreds of them from overseas and more than a thousand journalists altogether were gathered for the Gorbachev visit. For Deng Xiaoping, this was a great historic occasion — reconciliation between China and Russia. And since it was unthinkable not to hold the meeting at Tiananmen because of these students in the square, Deng insisted on going ahead. This, of course, gave the students an opportunity to demonstrate in front of the international media.

I was at that time in the United States to attend an international meeting of presidents of universities. We were meeting in California at that time, in San Francisco, and I had the interesting experience of meeting the President of Beijing University together with the President of National Taiwan University. All three of us were attending the same meeting and we even had a photograph taken of us. We were trying to communicate what we believed in about university education. But behind it all was this question of what was happening in Tiananmen Square, led by the students of Beijing University. I remember thinking that it was surprising that the President of Beijing University should have come, given the circumstances. In fact, he was not asked to rush back. He went on with a tour of the United States. I was told that eventually he was removed from office because the authorities wanted someone who was less sympathetic to the students.

What was his name?

The Beida president was Ding Shisun, a well-known mathematician and a Professor of Mathematics who was a graduate of Tsinghua University and also deputy chairman of the Chinese Democratic League, a close partner of the Chinese Communist Party. The situation was very complex. The Chinese government was taking a certain line, the students were taking a certain line, the international media were taking a certain line, and the presidents of universities were looking at all this with great concern. That the President of Beijing University was actually asked to stay out and continue on his journey in the United States suggests that there were complex factors at play. When I was still in the United States, it became quite clear that this was going to be very, very serious. But I had not expected what actually happened. Then I went back to Hong Kong and found that our students were demonstrating every week in the city centre streets.

Before leaving Hong Kong for the meeting in the United States, I used to meet my students. They too were asking for something reasonable like stopping corruption and inflation. The sympathy that they showed for the poor and the people who were directly affected by the inflation was to me perfectly legitimate. Indeed, Hong Kong students raised money for their counterparts in China. When I was away, Hong Kong students would march to show sympathy for Chinese students. Nobody did anything to prevent the raising of funds for the students in Tiananmen. The British did nothing or just kept an eye on what was happening; they played no other part. A lot of money was raised, and questions were asked about where the money was going, who was collecting it and who was keeping count.

By the end of May, there was a famous photograph of Zhao Ziyang speaking to the students, with Wen Jiabao

at his side. It was too late by then. The students, too, felt
that it was too late. But of course, this only intensified
their support, and from that time onwards, it was more
than just a few students: I think easily half a million
people in Hong Kong marched. It was no longer just
the students.

I was involved in the last stages of that eventful time
when we lost sight of some of our students for a few days.
Our students' union was engrossed in bringing money to
the students in China, and they were there even when
Tiananmen Square was cleared by the military. So we lost
sight of them for three or four days. Their parents were
calling, and we were all very alarmed. They came back
eventually. They had gone into hiding with their friends,
who were also friends of the Chinese students. That goes
to show the degree of involvement.

Some people have blamed the British for ruling Hong Kong
without democracy, and then introducing democracy just
before the handover to make life difficult for China in the
long run. Do you buy that argument?

Well, I don't know that that was the case. I think there were
several forces at work here. The British wanted to retain
some influence in Hong Kong. How to retain it, I think,
much engaged their best minds. One way of retaining it
was to have very good relations with China; that belongs
to one school of thought. But that earned them a lot of
international criticism, even from within Hong Kong, that
in order to protect their economic interests, they were
prepared to do deals with the communists and essentially

abandon to communist rule six million people who were living under a more open and free system. That criticism stung the British quite a lot because it was expressed within Europe and in the United States. They were criticized strongly by a lot of people who represented what they call the liberal democratic forces of the capitalist world, who asked what the British were doing to the people of Hong Kong.

Then, the Chinese were very demanding about what they expected of the British. The British were having a tough time negotiating their economic interests. That forced them to abstain from doing anything that would displease the Chinese.

The British were divided. There was no single agenda that everybody agreed on. British business people in Hong Kong were very unhappy with a lot of these policies because they were very concerned for their long-term interests. Why do you need any political adjustment here, they asked. This place is going to go back to China but the importance lies in our business relations with China.

The final decision was coloured by the concern that, when the British left — they knew they would have to leave — they didn't want to leave with their tail between their legs. It was a matter of national pride. That was genuine. They had to put up a show towards the end. I recall that, as soon after I arrived, there was this debate about the last Governor of Hong Kong not being a bureaucrat but a politician or a member of the royal family or some other significant figure so that there would not be just a routine, bureaucratic change of government. The ritualistic or ceremonial side revealed that it was important to British pride to leave with a sense of achievement, not with a sense of failure and defeat.

In the end, Tiananmen helped to resolve the issue to some extent. There was a complete Western boycott of China after Tiananmen. At least at the official level, all kinds of sanctions were introduced. Some are still in existence right now. So, in that context, the British decided to leave with their heads high. Therefore, they expected Governor David Wilson to push as much as he could for more concessions. It didn't matter whether this was ultimately realistic or not. On a matter of principle, they would push as far as they could to show that they cared for the people of Hong Kong, for their principles and for their belief in freedom and democracy. Even Governor Chris Patten, the next and last governor, at his most provocative did not expect the Chinese to give in on any of the issues that he pressed for. The issue was not that the Chinese would give in, but to go on pressing till the last moment so that the British could say that they had done their best up to the point when they left. That was the image they wanted to present at the end.

What are your hopes regarding Hong Kong's return to China in 1997? Have they been fulfilled?

There were different Chinas and it was by no means clear that China had a very clear picture of what Hong Kong would be like after the takeover. What was clear, though, was the underlying principle that they accepted the political autonomy of Hong Kong, a Special Administrative Region with its own Basic Law. I remember reading this quite carefully at that time and I actually believe that they were quite sincere about it, that they did want Hong Kong to be successful. Deng Xiaoping certainly was very clear. Now, not everybody in the Chinese government had the same picture of what Hong Kong should be like, but I think that Deng Xiaoping was quite clear that a separate kind of Hong Kong with a separate system while China was changing was actually good for China. It would help China in some ways. China could make use of Hong Kong, learn from it and have a kind of outlet for all kinds of feelings as well. There was no need for Hong Kong to conform because the last thing they wanted was a Hong Kong that was no different from any other city in China. The advantage of being different was that it had access to the world's resources and China could actually use Hong Kong for different purposes. So I think that, whether from the pragmatic or from the ideological point of view, Deng Xiaoping was very calculating and sensible about the future. I had no doubt in my mind that he meant it when he said: "50 years, no change."

Has that happened?

It's a slogan. How can there be no change? Especially in 50 years? There must be change. Once you change the equation, there must be changes. But the point is that there would be no sudden change, no complete change, no immediate sort of submission to Chinese wishes and so on. That, I thought, was true. They didn't want that. But the point is that it was impossible not to have some changes after Hong Kong had become a part of China. But they have kept to their word in the sense that they have not openly and directly intervened, as far as I can tell, in any decisions in Hong Kong. What they have done is to have their views put across to the Hong Kong leaders whom, of course, they have chosen, and allow them to do what they could to get these wishes accepted. But they have not pushed too hard and they have not pushed beyond a certain point. They have also taken into account the reactions of the Hong Kong people, on the very sensible and understandable principle that they see the importance of Hong Kong to China continuing for a long while. There is debate in China about how useful Hong Kong will be. Will it be less and less useful? But I think there is no doubt that Hong Kong will still be useful.

For example, initially, Hong Kong was seen as very useful to the country as a whole. It was China's window to the world. Over the years, this has become less and less so because China has found other outlets. There are Shanghai, Tianjin, Dalian and Beijing itself, and other cities that have their own networks and connections outside. So the whole country doesn't have the same need for Hong Kong. But it is also clearer that the South needs Hong Kong — the provinces in the south, particularly Guangdong province and Guangxi province. They benefit tremendously from the existence of Hong Kong even though they cannot control Hong Kong and Hong Kong doesn't depend on them. That relationship has been very valuable to those places. Now, that was not the intention. The intention was that Hong Kong would serve the whole country; Hong Kong saw it that way. But circumstances have changed.

This is one of the major changes: China is too big and it is growing so fast that it doesn't need Hong Kong in the same way as it did in the past. So now, the new role that Beijing is trying to work out for Hong Kong is that it is vital to the South, and more and more so given that the city helps the continual expansion and development of the South. But internationally, perhaps its financial services and educational services would remain always of value to the nation.

Hong Kong is adjusting to the new reality. It is becoming less of a national treasure and more of a regional treasure. But that is the reality, and both sides have adjusted very well. And I think this is the key to some of the debates of the time.

At the time of the handover, a lot of debates in the West hinged on how the communists would just swallow up Hong Kong, digest it and turn it into a Hong Kong corporation to deal with the world. Many people like myself didn't see it that way. We could see that the importance of Hong Kong to China would remain. How important might be arguable but it would remain important. The Chinese would find it in their interest to keep to the negotiated terms of 1983 and follow the Basic Law as closely as they could. That has turned out to be true.

China Rising

You have written about the fourth rise of China in the 20ᵗʰ century, after the Qin-Han unification of the first bureaucratic empire that lasted from the 3ʳᵈ century BC to the 3ʳᵈ century AD; the Sui-Tang reunification; and the

Ming and Qing dynasties. Do you expect China's fourth rise to be resilient?

When I used the words, "fourth rise", I was struck by the fact that China had finally overcome its period of decline. Historical analogies are useful for us to think in the very long terms, in which the Chinese people like to think anyway. China went through many periods of tumultuous disorganization, breakdown and break-up when the Chinese people were extremely weak and were hemmed in from all sides. But even during the long periods of division, there seemed always to have been the possibility of the Chinese reorganizing themselves and getting off the ground again as a unitary state.

The Han Dynasty represents about 300 years of great success followed by more than 300 years of division. After its breakdown, it was entirely possible for China to have become many different countries. There were many kingdoms and little empires, but it was basically a north-south divide, with the Yangtse River as the great divider. There were several dynasties in the north, and in the south. Eventually, the whole country came together again. How that happened is very dramatic. Underlying all those periods of division and brutal and deadly battles fought between so-called Chinese and so-called non-Chinese was the thread that they were fighting for the unity of China. That was ideological, the ideology being that there is only one heaven in the sky, there is only one sun in the sky. Hence, division is only temporary. So when unity was achieved, it was not something unexpected or unusual.

This took a long time to happen. When the Sui and then the Tang united the two halves of China after nearly 400 years of division, it was one sun in the sky again. In the rhetoric of all the Chinese thinkers, this was a glorious period when there were no longer civil wars. They stopped fighting each other and served one ruler for one ideal and one set of values. That became a part of the image of China, of what Chinese civilization is about — that China is essentially one and you may have periods of division but that all those responsible are almost duty-bound to bring the country together again sooner or later.

When the Tang Dynasty declined, the rhetoric of the Song Dynasty was to restore that greatness. But it never succeeded because, during the fall of the Tang, the foreign invaders had taken parts of north China. The Song Dynasty, while it united the whole of south China as well as parts of the north, never could quite drive out the Khitan forces from within the Great Wall and the Tangut from the northwestern territories that the Song considered to be part of a united China. There was continuous fighting. So although some Chinese historians might say that the Song Dynasty reunified the empire, it never really did. It was, in fact, on the defensive almost from the beginning and it stayed on the defensive. It lost territory, came to the south, and lost everything to the Mongols.

It was the Mongols who unified all of China again. But since the Mongols did not see themselves as a Chinese empire, I can't count that as a rise of China. Rather, it was the rise of the Mongols. However, the irony of it all is that because the Mongols unified China, they made it possible for the Chinese to take over from the Mongols a united China.

This was what occurred when the Ming Dynasty threw out the Mongols and inherited a country that the Mongols had united. For example, China now included Yunnan as a province, which had never been the case before, because the Mongols came through Yunnan to conquer China.

The Ming dynasty, having driven the Mongols out, inherited a united China under a Chinese emperor. This represented the third rise. It was succeeded by the Manchu 276 years later. One can argue whether the Manchu represented the fourth rise. Actually, the Manchu inherited the whole unified Chinese system. They fought the divided forces of the Ming dynasty. They killed a lot of people and the Chinese who fought back suffered badly from that invasion. There was desperate resistance for thirty or forty years but it was eventually wiped out. The Qing basically adopted all the institutions of the Ming to make themselves more acceptable to the Han Chinese. This allowed them to claim a part in the continuity of China. In that context, China's third rise lasted from the Ming down to the end of the 19th century.

What followed was the country's really serious decline from the end of 19th century to 1949. One can say that the decline lasted till the end of the 20th century.

Would you consider the Republican Revolution of 1911 to be a part of China's decline?

Yes, because the Republicans didn't do anything except get rid of the Manchu. The country was divided by military warlords. The Kuomintang never united China because it defeated only some of the warlords and controlled only a few provinces.

But did not the notion of a Republican China itself represent an advance in the Chinese history of ideas?

As an idea, that of a republic was certainly extraordinary. It replaced the monarchy. But it was never fully understood or put into practice, and certainly not in a united country. In fact, there was nothing but civil war from 1915, when Yuan Shikai failed in his bid to make himself emperor. But even from 1912, there was continuous civil war by different protagonists, and thereafter degrees of foreign intervention and invasion — by the Japanese and the Russians all the way down to 1949. It was almost one continuous civil war involving different protagonists fighting over different terrain.

So when did the fourth rise of China begin, precisely?

I didn't give it a date because 1949 didn't represent a clear rise. The Chinese continued to fight among themselves in a different way — ideologically — if not on the battlefield. In Mao Zedong's terms, the communists hadn't completed the unification of China. There were still Taiwan and Hong Kong. It was a transitional stage. It was only after Deng Xiaoping's reforms that China's fourth rise is apparent. The reconstitution of a united China has put the country on the way to a new manifestation.

Is China's fourth rise sustainable?

It is certainly more sustainable than anything before it. Much still depends on a communist party that is no longer based on any idealism and commitment to communism, and therefore has no ideological basis now except an appeal to some vague kind of socialism. It is neither here nor there because it is pretending to be a communist party while practising a variety of capitalism in which the bureaucracy plays an active part. It is using economic development to strengthen its control over the country, but development at this speed is costly for everybody.

Zhou Enlai famously said that it is too early to judge the French Revolution. Is it too early to judge the Chinese Revolution?

I think most historians, and this is my professional bias, would agree that you can't judge all these events anyway. We know from our study of history that new sources keep popping up and new perspectives keep cropping up. And as events unfold in time, future historians would have a different starting point and they would all want to look at the same events again. If you look at how much, for example, of Greek and Roman history has been rewritten in the past 100 years by the Germans, by the French, by the British, and by the Greeks and the Italians themselves, you see that each group may study the same thing but they ask different questions, not because the sources have increased much, but because they are possibly influenced by new disciplines, new academic fields, and new knowledge of other things that take them back and make them say: "C'mon, that explanation doesn't satisfy us, so let's have a look again." When you consider this, there is no period, whether it's the French Revolution or the Chinese Revolution, where you can make a real judgment. You can only say that, from your perspective today, this is what this revolution was about. That's okay in 2010 but in 2050, it may be quite different, and all your perspectives of 2010 will be shown to be very shallow because the world has changed.

This is something that we have learned to appreciate in the 20th century. Historians in the past were much more confident about their judgment. For example, in the 19th century, when the professional historian emerged and claimed a place in academia, they were convinced that it was a matter of getting the documents and writing the story. But, of course, we have learned since then that the documents are not reliable. What survived could be accidental; and what did not survive might be crucial. We began to realize the limitations of the documents. The fact that we have worked through all the archives doesn't mean that we've got the story right. We've got the story from the point of view of the archives, from what is collected in the archives. And who put them in the archives that determined the story that we are told? Now, we know that we don't know a lot of things.

For example, Chinese historiography was very clear. Chinese historiography was official historiography. It was done by the state for the Emperor and each dynasty did it. They actually had history officials to select the sources and write the history. With that in mind, what kind of history do you expect? There were resources that were preserved and anything that didn't fit their view was ignored, dropped, lost or destroyed — and we don't know what they were. There were, of course, anecdotes and miscellaneous stories that were told outside the palace and some of these were collected, but we don't know how to evaluate and use them. The Chinese have a term for it: "wild history" or "history in the wilderness", yeshi 野史. Surviving documents here and there may contradict the official story, but how reliable are they? Some of them might have been just rumour and gossip.

Chinese history has been rewritten completely again and again in the past 100 years by communists, non-communists, pro-Confucians, anti-Confucians, and so on. Given that, the Chinese Revolution has to suffer the same fate as any other event. It is subject to the vagaries of the sources and changes in world perspectives or political perspectives or professional perspectives. Economic, social and cultural factors, too, come in.

How did you feel when Mao Zedong died?

I must confess that I didn't feel any great sense of loss. I did feel that he was an historical figure of great importance to China, but I also felt that he had done so much damage to the country's traditions that it probably would have been better for China had he not been in power for so long.

He had done great service to China by the 1950s by producing a victory for his party, bringing about a kind of unification, and restoring China to a position that the Chinese people deserved. That was quite clear all through until the Cultural Revolution. I did think that the Cultural Revolution was something that he had to launch to satisfy his own vision for China, but I could not accept that encouraging the destruction of so much of Chinese culture was the way to serve that culture. Many slogans that had served him well during the civil war against the Kuomintang and foreign imperialists might have been justified during that period of history. But, those slogans were unjustified when they were extended, added to, and exaggerated into what became another civil war within the country.

I found it very difficult to understand his attitude towards the Soviet Union, too. I had no particular sympathy for the Soviet Union but I couldn't see how he could justify his own actions by moving on to the next stage of blaming everything on Khrushchev. He was standing on Stalin's side against Khrushchev and calling everybody who disagreed with him a kind of minor Khrushchev. That was irrational in my view. As early as that, I felt that he had passed the constructive stage of his life and had entered a very destructive stage. That he lived so long was tragic for the Chinese. This is the sad conclusion. Quite bluntly, his death was good for China.

A lawyer argues both side of a case but an historian argues both — or all — sides of a case and at once. What is the case for China today?

Well, the Communist Party argues the Communist Party's case very, very consistently no matter what other people think. It insists on putting across its point of view, which could be totally unacceptable to other people. Non-Communist Party members, even in China, do not necessarily accept the interpretation. So, among the Chinese themselves, there are numerous ways of writing their own history. And it's happening even now. You can see it today: different groups of Chinese perceive events quite differently. The official version is insistent that it is the only correct one and it continues to repeat itself. But it's interesting that even the official version now gets changed regularly. This reminds me of the famous saying about how the future is certain, the present is too short to know, and the past is changeable. You can rewrite the past. As the Soviets said, you can re-fix the past. You can retell the story, you can tell it in different ways, you can always manipulate the past. You can't manipulate the future because there's nothing to manipulate. The future was certain to them: communism.

Take the word "revolution". The Chinese accepted that the Japanese were right to have taken an ancient Chinese word to translate the idea of "revolution". The new use for that ancient word could actually refer to many kinds of "revolution". The ancient Chinese word, however, has its own connotations. When you put the two uses together and treat them as having one common meaning, then what happens is that the word now acquires a new meaning that can be applied to all of Chinese history, even though the modern word exists only from the end of the 19th century. You can now use this word "revolution", with all the modern ideas attached to it, and rewrite the whole of Chinese history, which is something quite extraordinary. But this has happened. The whole of Chinese history has been rewritten with the word "revolution" in its modern meaning, which never was there before, and is now used backwards in time.

What is the Chinese word?

Geming 革命. It actually means "to change the mandate". It was used by Confucians in that particular sense. Emperors and rulers and any aspirants to power used it to legitimize their regimes. But "revolution" is a foreign word to the Chinese. Now, the two words have been brought together and events have been renamed and history rewritten. What happens is that you use this word to say that revolution is a good thing, and anything that is not revolutionary is a bad thing. A peasant whose rebellion failed is a good guy because he represented revolutionary forces. And the guys who suppressed him are the bad guys. The whole of history is reversed. That history has been written to say that the man who imposes order, stops rebellions and so on is the good guy, not the other way round. In that sense, the Indians are very fortunate. They don't have a whole body of official history to correct by using a new word as the measure.

"Progress" is another such word. These are Western words that were brought into Chinese history, which has now been rewritten to reflect a new consciousness.

What is the Chinese equivalent of "freedom"?

Ziyou 自由.

Progress?

Jinbu 进步.

Equality?

Pingdeng 平等. These are the French Revolution's slogans! *Liberté, égalité, fraternité,* translated into Chinese, and are good words, like "democracy". But when you apply these words backwards, you ask yourself: What is history? How do you deal with the perspective of having a whole new vocabulary, a new rhetoric entering the picture? Everything in the past begins to look different because you are using different words. Language is very powerful. And even if you use your own language, once you have adopted the foreign word and taken it as your own, it affects everything that is in your own language. This has occurred clearly with China because no other country or civilization has this absolutely continuous story. Then you see that continuous story revamped totally.

A Western journalist once described post-1978 China as moving from Marxism-Leninism to Market-Leninism. Less dramatically, Beijing speaks of "socialism with Chinese characteristics". Does this formulation make ideological sense to you?

I think that these words are very deceptive and I find myself having some difficulty using them. To call it socialism doesn't match the definitions of socialism that other socialist countries use. But, then, the Chinese are very concerned not to be seen as capitalist. That's another word they reject.

Why is that?

Because that is linked to their hostility towards a system that was so closely associated with imperialism and that caused China to be weak for so long. In a way, they are still beholden to the Leninist interpretation of imperialism

as an extension and final form of capitalism. I don't accept
the interpretation, but it still has tremendous impact on
the Chinese. They didn't want to have anything to do
with capitalism. So they tried to rework their system in
terms of the modern scientific technology that the West
represents and has developed so successfully. They link
it to great economic development. This is the model that
they want.

However, they retain the word, "socialist", because
that's still a good word. Unlike "communism" or
"capitalism", with associations that neither side really
likes, socialism has never been rejected totally. Extremists
of the capitalist right reject it, but most people accept it
as being something benign, lying in between communism
and capitalism. The Chinese are comfortable with that.
They see socialism as being progressive, as opposed to
something reactionary. They would like to be associated
with something that's advancing and going forward and
becoming better.

Then, the question is: What kind of socialism? If we
use that word, we will have to give it some content. The
Chinese cannot accept a liberal-democratic socialism that
is rooted in liberal democracy and to which they would
have to be committed before they could proceed towards
genuine socialism. The Communist Party finds that it can't
accept that; at least, it is hesitant about that. So what it
wants to convey to its own people, if not to outsiders, is
that it wants socialism but is not prepared to copy other
people's socialism. It would have to be its own variety
of socialism: hence socialism with Chinese characteristics.
Also, the party doesn't want its socialism to sound very

nationalistic. Obviously, it doesn't want National Socialism [because of its Nazi connotations]. So it was brilliant of the party to think of a phrase like "Chinese characteristics", which softens the nationalist basis of its socialism.

What it actually will mean in the long run, I have no idea. I don't think Deng Xiaoping himself knew what it would eventually end up as. The phrase is a way of saying what the party doesn't want without actually knowing what it wants. The debates are going on.

Will China discover democracy with Chinese characteristics? Or will the Chinese political system be subverted by what Beijing has called "peaceful evolution", or the Western attempt to overthrow the system, not through force, as previously, but from within, through the peaceful invasion of liberal democracy?

The Chinese want something that is recognizably Chinese even though they do not know exactly what it is. And if democracy still represents something progressive that everybody wants, I don't think that they have any difficulty with that. What I think they would not want is a kind of slavish imitation of some democracy that has been developed elsewhere. They are sceptical about that because, having studied democratic societies, they seem to have come to the conclusion that some democracies evolve in such unique ways that they will not evolve on Chinese soil. That's like American democracy or European democracy. It comes out of particularistic historical experiences that cannot be reproduced in China. They don't see how China can move in that direction. As for other democracies that outsiders transplanted, for example in the Philippines, the

Chinese do not find the results impressive. They prefer to think of a democracy that emerges from China's own experiences over a period of time.

The communists have never rejected democracy. They have never said in their revolutionary literature that they don't want democracy. In fact, they believed that theirs was more democratic than the capitalist version, which merely represented the interests of the rich, whereas their democracy was meant for the poor. So the word, "democracy", is not a bad word in China. It is just that the Chinese want to find their own way of achieving something that all Chinese would agree to call democracy. In the meantime, they are not prepared to accept other people from outside telling them what democracy should be like.

Now, the Communist Party is not comfortable with a definition of democracy that assumes a whole set of other values as well. Some of those values are against the interests of the Party. Understandably, it does not want a democracy that would exclude it or drive it out of power. Hence, from its point of view, it wants to defend its interests and, over a long period of time, develop a kind of democracy that both the people and the Party can accept. This is what the Party is looking for. It's too early to say whether it can get it. At the moment, the whole thing hinges on its ability to perform.

Performance is an interesting concept. In a liberal democracy, people measure the government by its ability to perform, and they have the right to throw out a government and replace it by another one that they think can perform better. But that right presumes that everybody shares the same political values, differing only on policies. The

Chinese Communist Party knows that the vast bulk of the
Chinese people don't share its Communist Party values. And
since the values are not shared, the question of why the
Party is in charge becomes a very serious problem affecting
the legitimacy of the government itself. It is in a precarious
position where it does not want to experiment with any
kind of democracy that would threaten its existence. In
the meantime, it has to prove its legitimacy by delivering
on performance. Ever since Deng Xiaoping came back to
power, that standard of performance has been measured
by economic development. The party has been able to
deliver an average of over eight per cent growth per year
over the past thirty years. This means that it has to keep
performing at that level. The moment it fails to do so, it
loses legitimacy by its own standards.

Can it go on performing at eight per cent a year?
The Party is hammering that point to make sure that this
growth remains as long as possible. In the meantime, the
Chinese leadership is willing to see political reform so
long as it does not cause it to lose power. In my view,
every regime has the right to think like that. Is there
enough pressure from below to force it to undertake
political reforms sooner rather than later? This is a question
mark. But I think that political reform is definitely on the
agenda. The Party recognizes that. It can see that there
are serious problems in the way the government is run
today, in the way the so-called democratic process within
the Chinese Communist Party itself is not satisfactory
even to its own members.

Then, the way in which the central and provincial
governments are evaluating their relationship for the sake

of national unity reflects the genuine difficulties caused by the uneven development of the country. So eight per cent growth that does not relieve those inequalities: it actually adds to them. Somewhere along the line, political reforms will have to be undertaken to make people understand and accept the new situations, the new formations, the new rates of development, the new distributions of power and wealth. All these things have to be resolved to ensure legitimacy in the future.

For the moment, legitimacy is eight per cent, but that's no way to run a government for the longer term. You need shared ideals. You have to understand what the country is about, what it stands for, what its values are apart from money and wealth. What constitutes a civilization or a set of superior cultures gains respect when people believe that what it now offers is very, very good for everybody. And once they agree on that, they share those values. If the Chinese leadership cannot create a sense of belonging based on shared values, it's hard to see how it can assure itself of long-term stability.

How did you feel when you saw footage of a lone man standing in the way of the tanks in Tiananmen Square in 1989?

I recognised immediately that it was a very powerful symbol for those who wanted to show that the system deserved to be overthrown. I also thought that some of the interpretations by the Western press suggesting that the Beijing regime had had its day were overdone. However, the vast majority of the Chinese people never saw the footage. In any case, the idea that such an act could be interpreted to mark the beginning of the end of the system would not have impressed most Chinese. I belong to that group of people who would say that it was a powerful image. Young idealists might see that as an heroic effort by one individual. But I don't think that, even if they saw the footage, most Chinese living under the regime would read that much into it.

I was in Hong Kong at the time, and the people in Hong Kong were certainly strongly moved by what they saw. But we could not see what impact it had had on the Chinese people. The whole tragedy of Tiananmen, that six-week, seven-week period of standing up to the government and the government being paralyzed — that was most dramatic and it reflected something that was seriously wrong in the system. But, even at that time, while we were emotionally involved, we could see that there were limits to what a student uprising or demonstration of anger in Tiananmen could actually lead to. Did the students want to bring about the downfall of the communist government? I am not sure that they had that in mind. They simply wanted to show dissatisfaction with corruption and inflation. That's what they said openly and I think that's what they meant. But eventually, this was played out into something like a challenge to the whole system and an attempt to overthrow the Communist Party. And that, I think, was played up outside China as well.

In the end, this was about the Chinese being very pragmatic in their world-view. For something to be important in their eyes, it must have a consequence that makes a difference, something which leads to change that is tangible, visible and can be understood. No change came from Tiananmen, I'm very sad to say. If anything, things went the other way. And what had been very promising was cut off and there has never been another attempt to repeat it.

The Chinese government at that time knew of no other way to rectify the situation except by using repressive methods to control things, and it has been using those methods ever since. But it has used them fairly effectively because, let's face it, it has been able to control dissent and divert it into other things. People were angry but, very soon, they forgot about it. We are now talking about the generation of young people who don't even know, or talk, about Tiananmen. If you mention Tiananmen, they would have heard about it vaguely, but I am not aware of any sense among the young that this was a great moment that they want to relive and go back to. The government got most of the people working on developing the Chinese economy in ways that are really unbelievable. The critical question now is whether the economy can continue to grow at the rate the government feels secure with.

Turning to the international scene, although the Chinese government speaks in Westphalian terms, there has been some talk, including in scholarly circles, of 21ˢᵗ-century Nanyang resembling the tributary system that preserved peace and prosperity in pre-colonial Southeast Asia. Are such formulations fanciful?

I have seen writings about this for a long time. Much of what has been said, it seems to me, has drawn on very mixed pictures of what a tributary system meant. First of all, the Chinese never had a tributary system. That is to say, they didn't actually have a *system*. It was a set of feudal ceremonies and practices in the relationship between rulers that derived from a Chinese sense of the hierarchical nature of all politics. This is not peculiar at all to China. All countries had something like that. How a big country behaves towards a smaller country and *vice-versa* traditionally has been hierarchical. The idea of nations being equal is a very modern invention. It did not exist even in the League of Nations, when so much of the world was made up of colonies. The Chinese said essentially: You are the ruler of your polity, and I am the Emperor of China. I don't need to have anything much to do with you, but if you want to have a trading or other relationship with me, you have to follow these bureaucratic rules that apply to everyone. That's hierarchy. And when China was weak, it paid tribute, or something like it, to others. The notion of a system in which China forced everybody to pay it tribute is not true. There's no evidence of that at all. There was no system as such. Tribute was a symbol of the Chinese emperor's majesty, but it was primarily a mechanism to secure borders and ensure peaceful trading.

In this context, would you elaborate on your warning that the danger from a rising China lies, not in its looking back to its past, but in it trying to replicate the imperial pasts of the colonial powers in Asia?

Or America today. The fact that you are all-powerful and can go around interfering in other people's affairs is something that the Chinese have never done in the past. Will they do it in the future? Who knows, but it is interesting that the Chinese themselves are concerned about this. They made a whole series of films, "The Rise of the Great Powers". They tried to understand why these great powers rose because the principle on which the Western powers rose is something foreign to them. What is this principle? In China's heyday, it was the only great power in the region and it focused on defending its frontiers. Till the Europeans arrived, China had been invaded by ambitious foreigners overland. It built the Great Wall to deter them. The idea of setting out to colonize somebody else's territories and sending people there never occurred to the Chinese, as far as one can tell from their writings. For example, what the Westerners did in the Americas is something that never occurred to the Chinese.

You are saying that China was not an imperial power. This means, by definition, that it was not imperial outside China. However, others would argue that what China considered China to be was itself an imperial notion.

I know. These are interpretations that read back the kind of imperialist model that has come from the West into the Chinese experience. But, if you look at it from the Chinese side, they don't start from the same point. Yes, the Han Dynasty conquered the southerners. In fact, before the Han, the Qin had unified China and sent armies to the south and conquered the lands that eventually became provinces, like Fujian, Guangdong, Guangxi and An-nan (roughly the northern part of modern Vietnam). But then they stopped. Interestingly enough, that was when the Confucians appeared. When the Qin and the Han had conquered these territories, there had been no Confucians in the government. When the Confucians came into the government at the end of the 2nd century BC, they consistently advised the emperors against moving into territories that had nothing to do with Chinese civilization. They systematically emphasized the cultural unity of the Chinese and argued against imperial overreach.

There is the Southeast Asian example of Yunnan. Yunnan was a large and powerful independent kingdom until the Mongols destroyed the kingdom of Dali to get to China. They came down the upper reaches of the Yangzi into Yunnan and from there across poorly defended borders into China. The Chinese didn't expect it. They were always fighting the Mongols in the north and the northwest. Then Kublai Khan, a military genius, brought the soldiers down and attacked the Song Dynasty from the southwest and destroyed it. As I said, the Mongols united China and the Ming inherited it when they drove the Mongols out. Having inherited it, the Ming then took the new border as their border. Yunnan thus became a part of Ming China. But the Ming went no further.

The Mongols brought Yunnan into China, rather than China taking Yunnan.

That's right. No Chinese emperor could be said to have ruled over all of Yunnan until the end of the 14th century. If scholars made that clear, it would put the story in a correct historical perspective. Instead of saying that China took Yunnan, they could show how the Chinese inherited the Mongol Yuan province when the Mongols were finally defeated. After that, they set about to ensure that this strategic territory could never be used to attack China successfully again. Using the same analogy, China after 1911 inherited the Qing empire. What they inherited, they proposed to protect as their own. Is that imperialism? If these scholars want to call it imperialism, that's all right, but it was something quite different from what the West did when it sent people to the Americas, Australia and New Zealand, or when it seized territories in Asia and Africa. Perhaps what might be comparable is how Indonesia and India sought to inherit the borders of the Dutch and British empires.

The imperialisms were not of the same kind.

Not of the same kind. You could say that the Chinese, too, were in their own way imperialist. But you can't say that the Chinese were imperialist just as the Westerners were. I don't see the logic of using the same word to describe the different phenomena except as an attempt to defend Western imperialism by saying that the Chinese were imperialist as well.

Furthermore, unlike China's, Europe's was something modern. The imperialism after the 18th century was based on the emergence of what I call national imperialism — imperialism based on the rise of the nation-state. That was unknown in history because, in the past, all empires were built by feudal lords, whether Genghis Khan or Saladin or the Mughals. They captured and extended empires, but there was nothing national behind their empires. But when the post-Westphalia nation-state emerged in Holland, France, Spain and Britain, the first four nation-states, the empires that they built were national empires. They were first driven by mercantile capitalism, and then by the capitalism that had produced the Industrial Revolution. However, the idea of a nation-state extending its power by taking other people's territory, by using its own nationals to control the lives of the conquered, and exploiting these lands for the purposes of its own industrial revolution — that idea was totally new. That cannot be compared to the older imperialism.

Did China or India or anybody else in Asia do it? No. Nobody did that until Meiji and post-Meiji Japan. What did Japan do? Japan was carried away by the power of the Western national model. It thought that it could do the same and invaded China and Southeast Asia. Now, people are projecting that China could do the same. I am afraid that if the Chinese leaders get the wrong end of the stick, they could make the same mistake that the Japanese made. But I'm very encouraged by the fact that the Chinese are studying all this and realizing that it is not part of their tradition. It's not something they want to do. They have never done it and wouldn't know how to do it. And, if they try to do it, they will fall flat on their faces, quite frankly. I think that they are not going to do anything like that because they have learned from the fate of the nation-state empires. Even imperialism with Chinese characteristics will not be Western imperialism.

John King Fairbanks spoke of an historical Chinese world order. If that meant that the Chinese wanted to see order in the lands that bordered their self-contained Chinese world, that would be appropriate. But if the Chinese were thought to have conceived a world order that they would dominate, then no such world order existed. The concept of a world order is a Western one. The Chinese did have an idea of order that was hierarchical, one in which they saw themselves as the most civilized and the most developed. But theirs was not a concept of world order that led them to justify any kind of military intervention or the expansion of Chinese territory.

In that case, should the rest of the world be afraid of a resurgent China, or should China be afraid of a transitional world where powers in relative decline are armed nevertheless to their nuclear teeth? Who should be afraid of whom?

Throughout history, wherever there have been big countries and small countries, big countries have been feared. And big countries themselves have been fearful whenever they thought there was another big country around that could threaten them. It's like the idea of the fastest gun in the West, you know. The most dangerous thing is to be called the fastest gun in the West because there will be hundreds of people wanting to challenge you. You have to keep on testing yourself. To remain the fastest, you have to kill a lot of people. So, I'm afraid that that is true of all powerful countries. When they see other countries rising, it's very hard to resist the temptation to want to hit back and destroy them. And this would apply to any powerful country.

The Chinese were restrained by Confucian ideology because, for all its faults, it stood China in good stead by insisting on not pushing beyond frontiers, on the very realistic and practical grounds that if you can't control something, don't take it. Keep what you have and preserve it. Give order and provide civilization, culture and values. Don't bother with people whom you can't control and who are not like you. They don't want to be like you, so, leave them alone. Now, that was their virtue. By contrast, there is a kind of Faustian hubris in the much more aggressive nature of what I call the Mediterranean political consciousness, which is based on competition, rivalry and fighting each other to a standstill. From time to time, the Chinese had the power to dominate others but they restrained themselves. They have remained more or less within their boundaries for a long, long time.

China today is not powerful but it is big. Whether it is powerful or not, anything that big is frightening, just as I am afraid of an elephant although you may tell me that he is a gentle fellow and a vegetarian to boot. But I take one look at it and I'm fearful. I can't help it. For example, people talk about the Chinese economy becoming the equivalent of that of United States, but ordinary Chinese are actually poor. It's like that in India as well. It will be a long, long time before you can talk about Chinese and Indians being well off, whereas Americans and West Europeans *are* well off.

When you look at it that way, you see what happened when Germany was rising. The British and the French wanted to contain it. That's why, in the end, they fought two wars to try and stop the Germans. Finally, they pacified them. Perhaps that's the end of the story, but we don't know. Now, today, who is being challenged? The United States is being challenged. Would the U.S. let it happen? I don't know but, I mean, you can see the fear that it will not be Number One. The fastest gun won't be the fastest gun any more. Can you imagine that! So it wants to prevent this from occurring. Nobody in the State Department or the Pentagon would like to say: "At my watch, the United States began to decline." Everybody would like to say: "At the end of my period, we went up a notch." How do you prevent something occurring during your watch that meant that America began to decline? You have to do something about it.

Now, *that* is frightening. That, to me, is much more frightening than a rising power that has a long way to go. Both sides have reasons for playing the propaganda game. The Chinese are fearful of being stopped in their development. The Americans and other powers are fearful that China will become as powerful as they are or stop them from being overwhelmingly number one. And all countries have strategic planners who think like that. Whether there is a political leadership wise enough not to take unnecessary actions is hard to predict. I hope that every country will, in the end, have political leaders who won't listen to their alarmists and take them too seriously. But once there is an atmosphere of anxiety and concern, of being watchful and of being careful and continually worried and fearful, one miscalculation could make things go very wrong. So I would say that people have reason to fear a rising China, but Chinese leaders have probably more to fear from people who want to stop them from developing.

Is China being contained through strategic encirclement?
Can China be contained?

China has been contained militarily since the 19th century. Can it de-contain itself? The Chinese have been contained since the Opium War and were contained increasingly until the 20th century, when they were virtually strangled. They escaped from that strangulation but haven't escaped from containment. Nobody might be out to contain them openly but, then, the United States navy can sail cheerfully up and down the Chinese coast without objections from anybody, whereas if the Chinese navy were to sail up and down the United States' coast, it would be regarded as something horrific and horrendous. That doesn't sound right to the Chinese. But they understand that this is happening because of a kind of hierarchy at the moment, when there is only one superpower. The reality is that there has always been a hierarchy. The question is whether you recognize it legally or you don't, or you pretend that there's no hierarchy. The Chinese are practical. They will not do anything to give the United States an excuse to attack them. I am not suggesting the United States will do so, but the Chinese will not want to provoke the Americans. The question is whether the Chinese want to de-contain themselves. At the moment, they have no power to do so.

You have distinguished between the relatively benign nationalism of small countries that, because of their size and limited power, can hurt no one but themselves, and the belligerent nationalism of great powers that can rearrange the international scheme of things. If Chinese should not

*be nationalist, what can they be? Is there a tipping point
between defensive and offensive nationalism?*

What we call nationalism today is really very modern. In the
past, you had various kinds of loyalties. Some were tribal,
but that was a long, long time ago, except in places like
Afghanistan and parts of Africa. Most of the loyalties were
towards kings and monarchs — towards identifiable objects.
And they had limited range. But modern nationalism is a
very new thing. The Europeans have gone through it with
disastrous consequences for themselves, because they could
have dominated the world for another 200 years had they
not tried so hard to slaughter one another. Nationalism
destroyed them, as it did Japan. Germany and Japan learnt
that nationalism knows no other way to resolve a problem
except to try and defeat the other side. At least, this is
what their histories tell us.

I'm not defending nationalism even for small
countries. But I understand the need for it because, for
small countries, it is a question of how to survive. They
need some kind of cohesion, some kind of social cement
to hold people together. It can be quite positive to make
people feel proud of their country and so on. But it's very
dangerous for big countries because they cannot be certain
of controlling it.

Look at nationalism in China today. It is complex
because the Chinese people don't know how to be
nationalistic. They learned it only recently, in the past
100 years, after Sun Yat-sen. After all, they had Manchu
rulers, just like the Indians had Mughal rulers. What was
there to be nationalistic about? Indians were nationalistic

against the British for a while; in the end, the British went away and that has now faded. There are other reasons to be nationalistic and nationalism could be necessary for India for a long while. In the case of the Chinese, they, too, once had something to be nationalistic about. The Japanese invasion, in particular, was something about which the Chinese felt passionately because no other modern nation-state had really tried to conquer China. Generations of Chinese have found that attempt hard to forget. If Japan is clearly no longer a threat, there could come a time when that kind of nationalism could also fade away in China.

A really dangerous form that comes from arrogance could take its place. I don't think anyone can rule that out. And if a populist leader inclined that way should win legitimacy through democratic campaigns, that would be a great danger, in my view, to the integrity and survival of China itself. In addition, there is also a kind of demonstrative nationalism that could reflect the people's unhappiness with their own regime. They can't criticize it openly because there are so many controls on freedom. But they could show their anger by venting it on, for example, the Japanese or some other ostensible enemy.

I have the feeling that the Chinese people are still not really nationalistic. Theirs is not the nationalism of a genuine nation-state, which is truly shared because it involves the whole people. When a small country like Holland is threatened by large neighbours like France or Germany, all its people share the same feeling about their survival. That's totally understandable. But it is different in China or India. What do people share? They don't share an enemy — because most of their enemies are inside the country. For most people, the enemy is some corrupt official or stupid party leader or exploitative businessman. They are the enemies. So it would be bad for China if Chinese leaders make the mistake of arousing an external nationalism artificially. It would also be dangerous for the leaders themselves. I believe that they know this.

The most recognisable games of international life are perhaps football, cricket and hockey, with golf as a distant, well-to-do cousin. A case has even been made that golfing nations do not go to war. Which Asian game or games should now join the league of peace in the United Nations of Sport?

You know, the Chinese do very well in ping-pong, a safe game that does not kill anybody. Or badminton, another safe game. You don't get hurt, the way you could in rugby or even cricket. I suppose you could say that the Chinese shine in games that are individualistic, such as gymnastics or diving or swimming. They are not very good at team games. Their soccer is terrible. The greatest desire for the ordinary Chinese who love soccer is that they want a television set so that they can watch the Premier League. But their tragedy is that their national team is so poor, and their players do not seem capable of playing well together against anybody. Go to China and talk to any taxi driver. He will curse the soccer team because he's ashamed of it.

Unfortunately, the peaceful games that the Chinese are good at are not regarded as being very important. If

the dragon boat race can be developed, it may be the
Asian contribution to world sports. However, if it gets
competitive, perhaps it will get nasty too.

Taiwan, Japan and India

*What are some of the ways in which the Taiwan issue
might be resolved in the foreseeable future?*

There are probably two main outcomes rather than
resolutions because I'm not sure whether "resolution"
would be the right word. Outcomes are possible. One is
a long-term understanding reached between China and the
United States to leave the issue more or less as it is, in a
kind of *status quo* in which the Chinese will not make any
military moves and the United States will not do anything to
recognize Taiwanese independence. Beijing and Washington
would agree that this is a matter for China and Taiwan to
resolve one day — which is more or less the *status quo*
— but with the difference that both sides would acknowledge
more openly that they would leave the situation this way
indefinitely. However, such an outcome would depend on so
many variables that I'm not confident that it is sustainable.
There are many factors: the leadership in China, the
leadership in United States, but also developments within
Taiwan. None of these things is predictable because they
are each contingent on the others so that there are several
combinations and permutations there which are difficult to
calculate. But this is something that could last a long time,
largely because neither the United States nor China wants

to fight over this matter, and because Taiwan is prepared to accept that it does not have much choice since China's military takeover of Taiwan cannot be ruled out.

This cannot be ruled out because you could have a very aggressive group of leaders in China who have decided that the time for reunification has come because the Taiwanese leadership is getting difficult and seeking help from all over the world to recognize Taiwan as an independent state. However, I believe that this scenario is not likely because the ramifications would be immense; the costs would be enormous for everybody concerned.

The other outcome is that, eventually, the leadership on both sides would reach a point where younger leaders would take over and be less prepared to risk all just to be one country — reunification in the case of China, and independence in the case of Taiwan. They could negotiate about specific details and come to a lasting compromise. Taiwan's economic interests would be protected, China would not interfere in Taiwan's internal political affairs, and China's political interests would be ensured by Taiwan promising not to ally itself with a hostile country. Both sides would agree that China is one country but there is a set of leaders governing one republic and there is another ruling another republic. It doesn't sound feasible at the moment, and the question of nomenclature may be critical, but I wouldn't rule it out altogether.

Is the expression of a Taiwanese identity rather than a Chinese identity in Taiwan an impediment to the reunification of China?

Well, yes. The question of a Taiwanese identity is a question of usage. In China, there is a Shanghai identity, a Cantonese identity, a northerner identity, a Sichuanese identity, a Tibetan identity or a Mongol identity. All these are identities within one country. So for the Chinese to acknowledge that there is a Taiwanese identity is not itself that serious a problem, provided the Taiwanese don't deny that they are Chinese.

If identity were the only issue left, the Taiwanese would accept that they are Chinese. When the Taiwanese are in a good mood, they don't deny that they are Chinese. They just say that they are not the Chinese of the PRC. It depends on what you mean by "Chinese". If you use "Chinese" to mean a citizen of the People's Republic of China, they don't want to be that. But if you say "Chinese" in the sense that the Taiwanese speak Chinese, read Chinese, eat Chinese, celebrate all the Chinese festivals, and are culturally Chinese, they don't have problems with that. It's the political identity of being a PRC Chinese that they are not prepared to accept. The mainland Chinese are quite prepared to allow for a Taiwanese identity so long as it is not a nationality.

These are things that both sides can talk through but they need to have the right atmosphere, which must be rid of hostility, suspicion, fear or the feeling that one side is trying to destroy the other. Of course, Taiwan has no way of destroying China, but the thought that China would want to destroy the Taiwanese and turn them all into Chinese just like those in China leads them to seek foreign protection. The fact that they need foreign protection, of course, makes it very difficult for the PRC Chinese to trust them. Supposing that foreign protection comes from a power that is hostile to the People's Republic of China, where would the Taiwanese stand? That is the absolute test of what is feasible and acceptable. The PRC would never accept a Taiwan that was prepared to support a foreign state against it.

Turning to Japan, do you trust it to remain peaceful?

I have to believe that the majority of the Japanese people will never want war again. I am prepared to believe that. In every country, there are people who want war, people who are aggressive and expansionist. So it's a question of leadership, of political commitment and of internal economic and social development. I believe that the development of Japan since 1945 has created a society and a way of thought that would decry military exploits. I am prepared to believe that the majority of Japanese would not want to have any military confrontation with anybody. That does not rule out a few but I don't think they are the norm. So it's a manageable position by the Japanese leaders, provided, of course, that they, too, don't feel threatened, since all countries behave differently if they feel threatened. There is no reason for the Japanese to feel threatened except for the fact that there is a sense of insecurity arising from the fact that they have wronged other people, people who conceivably would want to take revenge one day if given the opportunity. These are unjustified fears. Eventually, I believe, fewer and fewer people would be fearful in that way.

The slight question mark that has been highlighted to me is that the Japanese have been taught to believe for 100 years that they are superior to their neighbours, including

the Chinese and the Koreans. They probably believed that
even before, but for 100 years or so, indoctrination codified
their sense of superiority. That superiority is measured by
their equality with the West. They thought that if they were
treated as equals by the West, they had made it. Hence they
put a lot of emphasis on achieving that equality so that the
Westerners would treat the Japanese as their equals. And
they were very proud when they achieved that, especially
after they defeated the Russians in 1904 and the West in
fact treated them as equals — as another great power. At
that point, China was on its knees. From Meiji down to
the 1950s, the Japanese did not believe that the Chinese
could be equal to them because they were so weak. This
sense is still part of Japanese culture. It will take some
time for the Japanese to change.

*Why does Japan find it so difficult to apologise to China
and Korea for its wartime past in a way that would bring
closure?*

It is related to the fact that the Japanese people believe
that they got into World War II because of the United
States, to whom they lost. They attacked Pearl Harbour
because the United States had been aggressive towards
them by denying them access to natural resources and, had
the Japanese not defended themselves, they would have
been squeezed to death. They wouldn't have continued
as a power. This is what Japanese textbooks say. This is
not credible. They forget why the United States took that
view. The reason, of course, was what the Japanese were
doing in China. Japan had been aggressive there ever since
their great victories in China in 1894–1895. Fifty years of

Japanese aggression in China provoked the United States into believing that it had to check that. The idea that the Japanese were provoked into the Pacific War and therefore that they should not be blamed simply doesn't cut any ice with most people who know any history. But this is something that many of their textbooks have said.

Then, of course, the war ended with the atom bomb, which gave the Japanese a kind of moral strength to have been the only people to have been so bombed. That element also makes it hard for them to want to apologize for a war that they believe they didn't start.

But there is the other side: the Korean and Chinese point of view, in which the Japanese were the aggressors from the beginning. Who attacked Japan? Certainly neither Korea nor China. Japan attacked them, and kept on attacking them. It enslaved the Koreans, took over Manchuria, and advanced into China. Many Japanese still try to avoid the issue. When they talk about the war, they concentrate on the Pacific War. Most of their textbooks talk about Pacific War and are very reluctant to admit that Japan invaded China. Even when they talk about the Chinese war, they often concentrate on the Marco Polo Bridge Incident. There are textbooks that suggest that it was the Chinese who fired the first shot. But why were those Japanese troops at Marco Polo Bridge, which is in China, in the first place? The way in which they rationalize these matters gives them a picture in which it is not at all clear in their own minds that they are to be blamed for any of those activities. There is a lot of Japanese literature from before the War in which Japan presented itself as fighting on behalf of Asians against Western imperialism. However, very few people believed Japan. I doubt that even

Subhas Chandra Bose really believed that the Japanese were trying to save the Indians from the British. That is part of their mythology.

When the War ended, the Americans decided to woo the Japanese by refusing to treat the Emperor as being guilty in any way. This was deliberate policy on the part of the White House, with General MacArthur implementing it. Washington was afraid of the Soviet Union's entry into Manchuria, its support for the Chinese in communist China and its support for North Korea. Winning over Japan and making it dependent on the United States was in America's interest in the long run. Then they would have a real foothold in East Asia, in addition to the Philippines. The net result of these American strategies was that, if the Emperor was not guilty, the people could not be guilty, either, because the people did what the Emperor had told them to do. Since the Emperor was not guilty and the people were not guilty, what is there to apologize for? So why are the Koreans and the Chinese being so unreasonable? Why do they keep asking for more each time the Japanese make apologetic sounds? The truth is that many Koreans and the Chinese do not feel that there was any real regret. And, as some would put it, what Japan regretted was that it had lost the war.

India and China are rising simultaneously for the first time since the onset of colonialism in Asia. What are your memories of the 1962 War between them?

The two peoples had virtually nothing to do with each other for centuries. For hundreds of years, Chinese

Buddhist monks went to India, developed a feeling for the Indian way of thinking and life, and took back to China the Buddhist sutras and other influences emanating from Buddhism. Ultimately, of course, that Buddhism became transformed into something very Chinese and was no longer recognizable to the Indians. But the fact was that the inspiration came from India. Beyond this, as I understand it, China and India were mutually irrelevant and were cut off by Turco-Mongol, Persian and other forces that created an area between China and India which kept them apart. Indeed, both sides were victims of these forces. So when peace and a resumption of relations broke out, so to speak, in the late 1940s, it was quite natural for someone like Nehru to be excited by the thought of a meaningful relationship between the two countries. It was also quite natural for the Chinese to be excited.

However, the difficult thing for the Chinese was the issue of Tibet's border. It came to a climax with the Dalai Lama escaping to India. India was trying hard not to offend the Chinese while accepting him as a religious leader in terms of a cultural relationship that the Indians could not deny. But the Chinese found it difficult to accept that the Indians would harbour somebody who, they thought, was escaping from their territory.

Who is not sympathetic towards the Dalai Lama? He's a man of tremendous wisdom and patience and is unbelievably good, like a Nelson Mandela. However, at the root of it all was the question of the border between India and China. If Tibet was a part of China — and Nehru acknowledged this — then, where do you draw the line? This is where ideological factors came in. Were colonial borders sacrosanct? The Chinese did not recognise the border that the British had drawn up as they had not been consulted when it was drawn. The Indians were prepared to accept the British border and hence the negotiations became increasingly acrimonious.

The Dalai Lama escaped when the PLA marched into Lhasa. The troops were massed in Tibet to keep control. Then the Chinese put them on the border, or what they considered the line of control. The Indians had no troops on their side. There were no proper roads and the whole place was hostile to human activity. You have to actually train for that. The Chinese had been training their troops for a long time, not to fight India but to control rebellious people. It was tragic that somewhere, somebody lost control and military action was taken.

The Indian army had no chance against the Chinese army in those circumstances. The political leadership failed very badly by putting the Indian army in that terrible position. If you want to talk tough, you had better be prepared. And if you are not prepared, then don't talk tough until you are ready. I think that the Chinese probably did not realize how poorly equipped the Indian army was and found it very easy to march down. But they didn't want to conquer India. They merely wanted to show that the border was something that they were not prepared to just give away but wanted to negotiate it. All they wanted to do at the time was to draw a line and negotiate for the area of Aksai Chin in the West. A deal could have been struck had there been some way for both sides to be more sensitive to each other's concerns and interests, and had more rational people sat down at the table to argue on first principles and make a sensible bargain.

What will be the consequences for Southeast Asia — a region named by its position south of China and east of India — should the two Asian powers drift apart?

First of all, let us hope for Southeast Asia's sake that they don't drift apart into any conflict. My own feeling is that if left to the Indian leadership and the Chinese leadership, there will not be serious conflict. Both sides have very rational leaders who recognize that it is not in the interest of their countries to have a conflict. There are no signs of hostility at the leadership level. There are signs of some caution, but neither side wants the situation to worsen.

Given this, I think that Southeast Asia can play a role in discouraging any drifting apart. The problem is whether forces from beyond the whole region want them to. I have written about the idea that, unlike India and China, there are countries that are very ideological now. India and China could be divided by using ideological arguments, for example, that one is on the side of the democracies and China is on the side of communism. ASEAN is in the best position to discourage this kind of division because it is itself not ideological. Being small, the ASEAN countries have no reason to be ideological. If India and China allow their own ideologues to link up with ideologues elsewhere, and to minimize ASEAN's role as an organization of small countries that are not important, matters will be different. Ideas of an arc of democracy or a league of democracies would make China

very uncomfortable. They would encourage the ideological
and more aggressive types inside China to come forward.
I do not wish that scenario on anybody. I do not rule it out,
but things are all right at the moment since pragmatism
now prevails.

The United States,
Terrorism and War

*Do you share the view that the United States is the
offshore balancer that helps to keep the peace between
China and Japan?*

That's taking a narrow, Southeast Asian point of view.
The United States is a superpower. By definition, a
superpower takes on responsibility for the whole world
and is active or is prepared to be active everywhere. At
least, by definition, a superpower is expected to take on
certain responsibilities. American internationalists believe
that their country's wealth and power compel the United
States to do some good. This is an idealistic and liberal
interpretation of a blessing. It is a burden as well, but one
that has to be shouldered. The United States is responsible
for helping keep international peace and ensuring its
own security. The two are not contradictory because the
security of the United States depends on its capacity to act
as a superpower successfully. So that is why when it is
challenged, and has not been so successful in some places,
it's a real anguish for it to know what it should do. Does

it continue to carry on a responsibility when it knows it is unable to do it without a lot of help? Should it resist the "America first" idea, which is the narrow-minded, realist view that America should look after its own interests and ensure only that nobody can threaten it? That debate is going on in the United States.

So when you say that America is an offshore balancer, that's speaking from a Southeast Asian or small-countries' point of view. It is not how Americans would see themselves. It's a very small part of "the city on the hill" idea, the inheritance of a manifest destiny. The United States can be expected to be helpful wherever it is needed and where it is wanted. If that is how those small countries out there want the United States to participate in their security against big powers in the neighbourhood, like China or Japan or India, the Americans can be expected to do their best. But this point of view has its limits. It would be a mistake to call it an offshore balancer. The smaller countries shouldn't calculate on that basis but essentially appeal to the American vision if they want the Americans to be around and to take on responsibilities that have nothing to do with American security but has to do with American prestige and superpower status in the world.

Post-Iraq, what would be the effects of declining American influence in Southeast Asia?

I'm not sure that post-Iraq and post-Afghanistan, for the two are linked, American influence in Southeast Asia would necessarily decline. Even if they do not bring about peace in those two countries, their capacities elsewhere will not be necessarily diminished. So the question is not so much a decline, as whether the American people might decide to pull back from commitments that have nothing to do with their security *per se*. If that argument wins the day, then the issue will not be their declining influence but their unwillingness to take on things that do not touch on their key interests.

So the essence of the question would be: would the Americans still see Southeast Asia as being essential to their interests? My feeling is that they will because it has nothing to do with Iraq or Afghanistan. It is a completely separate interest born of America's position in the Pacific. It needs peace on the opposite side of the Pacific to be secure itself. After Pearl Harbour, the military balance began to shift towards the west coast of the United States. The Cold War was centred in Europe, and so the Americans had to continue their presence in Europe on a much bigger scale than in the Pacific. It was the end of the Cold War that made it clear that the whole balance had shifted. Europeans could look after themselves and, therefore, American attention turned to the Pacific. That decision was a strategic, long-term one. Since the western Pacific means Southeast Asia plus China, the Koreas and Japan, they will never lose interest in this area. It is vital to their national security.

What are some of the ways in which terrorism can be tackled in the long term?

Over time, terrorism has subsided in some areas. Certain negotiations have been carried out patiently over many decades, certain ends have been achieved, and certain compromises have been made. Ireland comes to mind here. There is no single formula in finding a solution. What have helped are expertise, local knowledge, a willingness to negotiate peacefully, and a capacity to hold back from the use of extreme force except where necessary. Terrorism today is not about Islam being ranged against the Christian powers. Nor is it purely a matter of poverty. There are ideological issues that have to be taken into account. The terrorists don't come from the poor. The poor are not in the position to be terrorists. The terrorists usually come from people who know something about the issues and can take look at the bigger picture for which it is worth sacrificing their lives. They employ skills, organization, sophistication, knowledge of weaponry, and an understanding of international markets to get weapons

Except for fanatics with whom you cannot talk, most of these people can see reason and give and take. They resort to terrorism only when they think that there is no other way of achieving their ends. If they can be persuaded that there are, indeed, other means, there would be no need for them to sacrifice hundreds of young people. But you have to persuade them that there are other ways that are feasible, achievable and can be acceptable to them. That calls for negotiation. In the meantime, violence on both sides is probably unavoidable because both are trying to achieve a better negotiating position before they sit down to talk. Until one side or the other feels that that position has been reached, it cannot sit down. I think that it is very tragic if either side believes that the only way to solve the problem is to destroy the other.

As a non-Muslim, are you worried by the dream of a Calpihate stretching from Cairo to Aceh?

I don't see an old Caliphate emerging. If a Caliphate came about, it would have to be a very different one, based on a modern understanding of global economics and politics. To return to a medieval — I would use the word deliberately — concept of the Caliphate going back to the days of the Umayyad won't do. Even the Caliphate of the Ottoman Empire was a vague concept. It had no substance.

However, the idea of an *umma* whose Muslims consult and defend one another is a legitimate one. It is perfectly legitimate to protect a religion. The commonalities of a religious life that are expressed in humanistic terms are not only legitimate but are to be welcomed.

It has been said that war is inevitable, but the next war is not. What do you think?

As an historian, I take the view that war is inevitable. I have no evidence that war can be prevented completely. War is the measure of the failure of peaceful efforts to solve problems. The conflict might not involve fighting, but it will take the form of struggle. That is normal because humans have misconceptions, they miscalculate, they can be paranoid, they can be psychotic, they can be megalomaniac, and they make mistakes. War cannot be avoided unless you can devise a system that prevents such humans from becoming powerful enough to declare war.

Some people argue that democracy prevents war by electing mediocrities to power. Democracies don't go to war with one another. If everybody were rational, the democratic peace theory would probably be better than any other theory that I have heard of. However, democracy as a theory is one thing. The kind of institutions that democracies have established in different parts of the world, which are rooted in different locations, histories, cultures and value systems, makes it impossible to guarantee that the people will be wise always. There are populists who are capable of using the democratic system to arouse passions that bring out the worst in people. The best in people would reasonably bring up leaders who would never go to war, but the worst in people would do precisely that, by bringing to power someone who could passionately arouse them to believe that war was the best solution for their problems. We have seen that. Aristotle used historical examples to show how democracies could bring about a populist dictator who then took a people into war. No political system I know can guarantee that it will produce people who will always work for peace.

Half a Century of Marriage: An Interview with Mrs Margaret Wang

When, where and how did you meet Professor Wang?

We met in 1951 at the University of Malaya. In those days, the university was at the Bukit Timah campus. He was only a year ahead of me because, when he came back from China, his one and a half years there were not recognized. He had to start as a freshman all over again. So although he is three years older than me, we were only one year apart in the university.

How do you remember your first meeting?

We were both on the Students' Council. He was the president of the Students' Union and I was one of the council members. He asked me out to the pictures after one of the meetings. I remember it very clearly: it was Macbeth with Orson Welles as Macbeth.

So, he made the first approach.

Oh yes. But I must confess that I didn't run very fast when he started to chase me!

How did the relationship develop after that?

Well, I suppose you could say that we became boyfriend and girlfriend. We didn't have very much money so we did simple things like going for walks, seeing some good films and eating at roadside stalls. We found that we enjoyed the same sort of films, books and music. We got to know each other quite well during those years of courtship.

Then what happened?

What happened was that he decided to study history. For an academic career, he needed to get a higher degree like a Ph.D. So if he went to England, what would happen to us? We decided we'd get engaged. He would go to England and I would stay behind for a year, work and save some money because I felt that my mother, who was the sole supporter of my family, should not be burdened any more by a daughter who didn't earn any money. So I went to work; I found a job at St. Andrew's Boys' School. It was looking for an English teacher for the sixth form. I went to be interviewed and was hired on the spot. I never intended to be a teacher. I became one nevertheless when I realized I enjoyed teaching very much.

So you followed him to London later?

Yes, but I actually didn't go to London, I went to Cambridge. I'd heard of Homerton College in Cambridge through a friend of mine who was going there. Homerton College trained women to be teachers and offered a one-year Post-graduate Certificate in Education course for graduates. Gungwu was at that time in Cambridge. His thesis supervisor had moved from London to Cambridge so Gungwu went to Cambridge too. And he said: "Why don't you come to Cambridge because it's a lovely town to be in?" I agreed. Then we found out after I had completed all the paperwork and so on that he couldn't actually stay in Cambridge for more than a year. Those were the residential rules for Ph.D. students. So he went back to London and we were once more separated. We spent the first term of my year commuting between London and Cambridge. Both of us got tired of it as all our weekends were spent travelling between Cambridge and London.

Then he said: "Why don't we get married?"

Wonderful!

We were already engaged so it seemed quite logical for us to marry. It helped that his parents were in London at that time and could give us parental support. So we got married in London in December 1955. We found a flat and lived in Cambridge until I finished my course. Gungwu's supervisor was kind enough to shut his eyes to the fact that Gungwu wasn't supposed to be in Cambridge. We returned to Singapore in 1957 after he had completed his Ph.D.

Is it true that you have never had a quarrel in all these years?

No, not true. That is simply not possible in such a long marriage and neither of us is a saint! I quarrelled, but he didn't. You can't quarrel with a person who doesn't quarrel back. So after a while, we, or rather I, stopped quarrelling. He had never heard his parents quarrelling and so didn't know how to quarrel. I am the kind who is quick to anger but I forget it in two minutes. So, provided you tolerate my outburst and don't say anything, the whole matter actually goes away very fast. However, that doesn't mean that we don't have disagreements now and then.

Interesting!

Actually, we are temperamentally very different. He's very relaxed, very patient, very tolerant. I'm impatient. I want things to be done instantly and I'm a bit of a perfectionist. So, you can see the seeds of a lot of dissension. But because he didn't quarrel, it made me feel so foolish whenever I got angry about something that my anger never lasted long.

Was that a Confucian pact?

Oh, no. I'm not a supporter of Confucianism. There are many good things about Confucianism but the philosophy and system are very male-oriented and Chinese women suffered under it for centuries. I'm very much for women's rights. But Gungwu is actually in the enviable position of being able to do something about it. He employed women whenever he could and encouraged his female students to take up scholarships to do higher degrees. He has always shown great respect for women and I admire that. I'm the beneficiary of this attitude because he always treats me with courtesy. That's how his parents treated each other.

His parents had an arranged marriage so they had to work at it much harder than other people. They were not in love or anything like that when they married. But they showed great courtesy towards each other, and their marriage was marked by a certain standard of behaviour that was very civilized. In the end, they grew to love each other very much. His father was a real Confucian gentleman in the best sense of the word.

But I wasn't brought up as a Confucian. I was brought up as Methodist — a Christian!

How many brothers and sisters do you have?

Three brothers and one sister.

When were your own children born?

They were born in April 1957, July 1959, and April 1961. Two years apart. I think couples of our generation tended to marry young and have our families young.

So you went back to work?

Yes. St. Andrew's needed a teacher in English language and literature for the Sixth Form once again and the headmaster wrote to me while we were still in England asking me to rejoin the school. We arrived in Singapore on a Wednesday or something like that. And, by next Monday, I was back at work. We moved into a flat provided by the university. I remember scrubbing and cleaning it. When you are young, you can take a lot of hassle.

You must have had to change jobs as Professor Wang went from place to place.

Because of Gungwu's moving about, I lost many jobs, and some of them were quite good ones. It's a choice one has to make. I always agreed to every move we made. He discussed things with me and we would weigh the repercussions of each move. We have a very good marriage in that sense. And I must say that each move added a new layer of experiences to our marriage.

In Australia, I learnt to wield the electric drill and other tools you need to put up things in the house. Well, I could not wait for him to come back and do whatever needed to be done.

As I told you, I am a very impatient person. I preferred to do things myself. I built bookcases, put up shelves and I learnt how to cook. I enjoyed gardening and grew roses as well as vegetables. When we first went to Australia, I didn't work because our children were very small and I didn't want them to come back to an empty house. So I decided not to work. This lasted about six weeks.

Then I said to Gungwu that I just couldn't bear not working. It was so boring to be at home all the time just doing housework. So he said: "Why don't you go back to school, do another degree?" I said: "What a good idea." So I immediately signed up for another degree and I kept myself happily occupied mentally for four years. I did an honours degree in Asian Studies at the ANU. After I finished, I looked at my children: they were physically all bigger than me! The eldest was in his teens by that time, and so I went back to work.

Where did you work?

At the Canberra College of Advanced Education, which is now Canberra University. I finished my degree in 1972 and, in 1973, the Australian government recognized China. Immediately, there was an offer of five scholarships a year to five Chinese students to come and learn English.

The Chinese government managed to squeeze 15 students into those five scholarships. So suddenly, we were faced with an influx of people from China. There was this TESL (Teaching English as a Second Language) department at the College, which was going to teach the Chinese students. I was appointed one of the tutors for this group. So I started working, teaching English again. My specialty was English as a Second or Foreign Language. It was what I had done in Kuala Lumpur. It was part-time in the sense that I worked for only about 12 hours a week. It meant that I could go home in between classes if the children were sick or needed me. It was an ideal job for a woman with young children. And I didn't come home so exhausted that I couldn't talk to my children. I enjoyed the teaching very much because our department expanded to teach anyone at the tertiary level who needed to improve their English. Our students were not only from China. We had Cambodians, Vietnamese, Thais, some Europeans, South Korean civil servants and so on.

When Professor Wang went to Hong Kong as Vice-Chancellor, did you work?

I could have worked but it would have been difficult. I couldn't work at the university. He was its head and people would criticize him for that. Anyway, being a Vice-Chancellor's wife is busy enough. You have to organize big receptions, dinner parties, lunches, talk to people who are total strangers, talk to the wives, and make everyone feel comfortable in your home.

So after Hong Kong, it was back to Singapore.

Well, actually, we never intended to come to Singapore and were going back to Australia. But when Chan Heng Chee heard that Gungwu was going to retire, she asked him to join ISEAS as a visiting Professorial Fellow for a year or so. And then, [Goh] Keng Swee wrote to him and asked whether he would like to come to Singapore to take over the chairmanship of the IEAPE. I didn't want to go back to Canberra at that time. I wanted to live in Asia. I have always felt most at home in this part of the world. So I said: "Singapore seems ideal." This time, I was the one who made the decision to move!

Where are your children now?

Our son is in Sydney. He was in Singapore for about ten years until two years ago. Sydney University, his alma mater, established an endowed Chair in Radiology and invited him to fill the position. So he went back. One of our daughters, the one with two daughters, lives in France and is married to an Australian, a recognized expert on road safety who works in a research institute in Lyon. Our third child is in Melbourne. She works as the Publishing Manager at the Australian Institute of Family Studies. We are a close-knit family and communicate several times a week via Skype, email or telephone.

What has life given you and Professor Wang?

We both feel that we have been extremely lucky in our life together. Firstly, we have a wonderful family. Our children and grandchildren have given us great happiness and are a source of pride to us. Early on, I realized that I was not going to be married to a nine-to-five man, and so I have learned to be adaptable. We have lived a very busy and productive life. We have met very interesting people and Gungwu has had some great colleagues. We've lived in all sorts of countries and have friends from all over the world. I would say that we have lived a very rich life and continue to do so. We have had a very good marriage of 54 years, going on to 55, and we continue to enjoy talking to each other. We still have plenty of conversations ahead of us!

APPENDICES

In Conversation with Professor Wang Gung Wu
by Vineeta Sinha

ISA E-Bulletin, no. 6, March 2007, pp. 27–38

Vineeta Sinha (VS): *Thank you very much for this opportunity. I would like to begin by talking about your contribution to research on Chinese history and migration. How did you come to this field in the first place?*

Wang Gungwu (WGW): I took my first degree in the University of Malaya, when it was in Singapore. It was a very small, new university, formed by merging Raffles College and the King Edward VII College of Medicine. The number of subjects available to the Arts students was very limited. We really had very few choices. For quite a few years, all we could choose from were the four subjects, English literature, history, geography and economics. The university followed the system whereby students did three subjects for a general degree and then, in the fourth year, if you are admitted into the honors class, you could specialize in one subject. In my case, I was given the choice of the three: English, history or economics. I was uncertain which to choose. My personal preference was for literature but the practical thing to do would have been to do economics. I did work at my economics courses and did like much of it. I thought history was an interesting subject to be studied for its own sake but in career terms, economics was the practical thing and my fellow students thought that as well. Literature was my private love. In the end I didn't do economics. I was admitted to the honours class but, frankly, thought that the professor of history was far more interesting. His name was Cyril Northcote Parkinson. He was responsible for the Parkinson's Law that is now part of the language of administration and management. And he was really a fascinating person. He was a naval historian but not at all conventional. Although his whole career up to the point I knew him was straight naval history, Anglo-French naval, battles, in the Indian Ocean and elsewhere, in fact, whenever he taught us, he was extremely stimulating. The three lecturers who taught me history in my first three years were also inspiring, so that too encouraged me to take history. When I saw that Parkinson was going to be the man in charge of the honours class, I thought that a year with him would be intellectually far more satisfying. One of the reasons why I didn't do English literature was also because the professor, Graham Hough, had left. He was very good but he left to take a job in Cambridge. We lost him, hence my decision not to go further with English Literature. But I was not someone who set out to do history from the beginning. I actually did poorly in history at school and just barely managed to pass. And I remember when I came to register for history, the history lecturer who was registering me looked at my results and said, don't you think you should be doing geography or something? I had actually done better in geography in school. Anyway, I didn't take his advice and in the end it was history that turned out to be the subject that interested me.

VS: *How did you become interested in Chinese history?*

WGW: I had actually gone to China for higher studies. My first university was in China. After I finished school in Ipoh, I went to take the entrance examinations to the National Central University in Nanjing, in 1947, and was offered a place in that university. I was there for a year and a half. When the communists arrived, and civil war was going to engulf the city, Nanjing was abandoned and the university closed. I hung around the campus for more than a month, but my parents persuaded me to come home. So I did. I had already done the first year in Nanjing and was in my second year. What I saw of the tail-end of the Chinese civil war was another factor that influenced my later interest in history. When I decided to do history, the context at that time saw a shift towards the history of the West in Asia, from the early interactions to the growing dominance of Asia by the West. This reminds me that, just about the time I completed my history honours year, KM Panikkar brought out his *Asia and Western Dominance* where he wrote about the Vasco Da Gama epoch of Asian history. My understanding of Asian history at that point was that Asian states were still very much alive and kicking until the late eighteenth or early nineteenth century. It wasn't till the nineteenth century that the Europeans really began to dominate. Before that, they were largely controlling some islands and clinging onto bits of coastal land. During the first three centuries after Da Gama reached India, they did become more influential but were not dominant. And the Europeans were fighting amongst themselves as well as fighting Asian powers. For most of that time, they were actually quite respectful of Asian cultures and did not see themselves as superior. It was only in the nineteenth century, after the Industrial Revolution, that they obtained the extra economic power to translate commercial preeminence into military and political superiority. That was what gave them the edge and, from then onwards, Asia did not have a chance against them.

The European powers had also learnt from their experience in Asia. They learnt to stop fighting one another and decided to carve out spheres of influence to avoid unnecessary fighting among themselves. And that gave them even greater opportunities to dominate whatever territories that each power had carved out. The Dutch in Indonesia or Netherlands East Indies, the British in India and later Burma and Malaya, and so on. They stopped fighting each other by the beginning of the nineteenth century. The last great struggle was the Anglo-French battles of the Napoleonic era, after which the British became the number one power. So Western dominance really came about only during the late eighteenth and early nineteenth century. KM Panikkar was right, the Europeans became dominant, but it was too early to date it from Vasco Da Gama. Vasco Da Gama was barely clinging to bits of Cochin and Calicut. On the contrary, I thought that, between Vasco Da Gama's arrival in India down to the eighteenth century, Manchu China was actually still very strong and had actually expanded its empire into Central Asia.

So I was interested in how the Chinese eventually recovered from that period of western dominance and how a new China came into being in our time. When

Mao Zedong announced that China had stood up on the first of October 1949, that was just a week before I became an undergraduate at the University of Malaya. That is a week I cannot forget! I was thinking, how did these Chinese become Communists? What is in Chinese tradition that would make them Communist? How could they have enabled the Chinese Communist Party to defeat the Nationalists immediately after a war against Japan during which the Nationalists had become powerful? It was a time when these Nationalists were, if not at the peak of their power, at least enjoying the triumphs of heightened nationalism. How could these Communists have defeated the Nationalists? That was already one of the questions about Chinese history that interested me. Related closely to this, of course, was another question, how could this great civilization of 2000 years collapse to a point when the Chinese people were no longer confident of their own civilization? And many young Chinese were indeed no longer proud of their civilization and were prepared to abandon it. In the 1920s and 30s, young intellectuals in China were saying, "Out with all this feudal, traditional nonsense, we must be progressive, we must learn from the West, we must take their new ideas and transform ourselves into a rich and powerful country". Why would people say that? So that's where I started, my starting-point, so to speak.

Unfortunately, in 1953, when I was doing my honours year, the conditions in British Malaya, of fighting communism, of Emergency regulations being in force and the high degree of surveillance of the people, there was no way I could have done Chinese history seriously. All

Chinese were suspected of being communists, the way that
all Muslims are suspected of being terrorists today. It is
very similar. I find it familiar when compared to the way
we young Chinese at that time were suspect, especially
someone who could read and write Chinese and had been to
China. As far as the British and the Malayan governments,
all the government officials and police officers, were
concerned, we were all suspicious. So I couldn't seriously
do work on modern China without all kinds of difficulties.
I was not an anti-communist, not ideological in that way.
If anything, I was more sympathetic to those people who
were idealistic about what they were doing. It turned
out badly for these idealists in the end but, at the time,
I admired them for the sacrifices they were prepared to
make to try to achieve what they wanted.

But the atmosphere was just wrong for the kind of
history that first interested me. Although I started out with
modern China, by the time I decided to do my Masters
degree, it was quite clear that that would not be possible.
As for my professor, he basically said that he would
support me but I should know the difficulties here. So
I shifted to the history of Asian trade. I decided to work on
the Nanhai trade and went back in time to study Chinese
trading relations in the South China Seas. I actually went
back 2000 years and wrote my Master's thesis on the first
thousand years, from the Han dynasty down to the tenth
century. Well, that was politically correct, no problems,
and I could also use that opportunity to learn early
Chinese history thoroughly. There was nobody to teach me,
so I had to learn what I could by myself.

The university's library was quite inadequate, but
I was a bit fortunate in that, just as I was about to start

on my work, the university established the Department of Chinese Studies. They did so not because they were that keen on China. They did that because of the pressure put on the colonial government to allow the Malayan Chinese to found Nanyang University now that Chinese school students could not further their studies in Communist China. Again, the context was local politics. The British were very concerned that, if they resisted that pressure all the way, they would have a rebellion on their hands and the young Chinese school students would then become even more left wing and radical. So it was a kind of politics of concession but also politics of contention. The British were very unwilling to allow the foundation of Nanyang University, so they created the Chinese department in the hope of satisfying local demands, that is, by enabling Chinese school graduates to do Chinese at the University of Malaya. But the Chinese were too clever to accept that. They recognized that it was a diversionary move and they really wanted their own university. So finally the British gave in and allowed a Chinese language university that was privately funded. But they were not keen on it and only allowed the community to set up a company to run the university. The politics of that whole affair was extremely complicated. But, as a result, the Chinese department was set up at the University of Malaya, and it began to buy Chinese books for the library, of course, mainly traditional books. That was fine for me, since I was pursuing a traditional subject for the first thousand years of the millennium. So I had the basic reference sources to work with and that enabled me to complete my Masters. When I went on to do my PhD, I had hoped to go beyond that and get into more recent history. As it turned out, since I was still trying to learn more about Chinese history, and there was still so much more to learn, and I was finding pre-modern history very interesting, I decided to continue in that field. When I went to London and met a scholar who was willing to supervise me and found him keen to encourage me, that clinched it. Thus the tenth century became the focus of my PhD research. That's how I landed in "medieval" history, to use this very European term to cover my research period.

When I finished that work and came back to Malaya to teach, I knew I was handicapped in many ways. I had limited social science exposure, did not have the kind of classical training that the humanities would normally expect. My modern history training, when applied to the study of ancient times, wasn't really helpful. Furthermore, I also didn't have a chance to hone my skills in modern history research. So I really had much to do to make up for my shortcomings.

VS: *But one could also say that you were liberated, because you were not bound by the constraints of disciplinary knowledge and therefore you were free to carve your own...*

WGW: That would be a positive interpretation of a rather unfortunate set of circumstances! Yes, I suppose, in the end, I didn't lose anything, I gained a depth of understanding of the past which helped me later on when I came back to modern times. When I came back to teach in the university, I was assigned to teach the period from the beginnings of Western impact on Asia to the time of Western dominance, mainly the 16th to 18th centuries, and teach what was Asia's response; in short, what was happening in Asia at that time. I was given the job of handling that period of East Asian history, especially China. Which was fine, it suited me very well because it gave me a chance to get a bit closer to modern times. It was China from the 1500 to about 1800, and gave me a chance to learn more about that period. I enjoyed that enormously, I have always learnt so much from teaching.

VS: *Yes. This was in Hong Kong?*

WGW: No, that was here at the University of Malaya in Singapore. This is where I came back to, this Bukit Timah campus, not exactly in this building but the one just around the corner next to the present Faculty of Law main office. I had been here as an undergraduate, and then taught here as well. But in 1959, they started the campus in Kuala Lumpur and, because I was a Malayan and Singapore was still a colony then, I thought I would like to join that brand new campus. They asked for volunteers and I asked to go to KL. As a result, I left Singapore in 1959 and didn't come back till 1996. It was a long gap. I was in Kuala Lumpur for about eleven years and then after that I went to the Australian National University in Canberra.

Not long after I got to Kuala Lumpur, the capital of the newly independent Federation of Malaya, I became head of department and professor of history, and it became quite clear that I would need to concentrate on Southeast Asian and Malaysian history. That also gave me the chance to teach modern history, especially that of Malaya and the region. All my students, especially the students I was supervising, were doing either Malaysian history or Southeast Asian history. Such subjects were very much at the core of our department's courses. In addition, I had also developed a particular interest in teaching the theory and method of history and that was why I became interested in the social sciences. When I began to teach theory, it was obvious that historians on the whole didn't talk much about theory. They were probably wise not to have done that and leave it to the philosophers. So I really had to turn to other disciplines for guidance. It was very stimulating to look at the theoretical work done in related fields, ideas and methods that historians were actually using, often without acknowledgement and sometimes without a clear understanding. Nevertheless, there was a growing recognition that what these disciplines brought forth was actually very helpful to historians and historians should become more self-aware about what they were doing.

VS: *Could you mention some of these works that pulled you into Social Science theory?*

WGW: Normally with these courses you teach historiography, and begin with all the work done by historians in the past. Herodotus and Thucydides in Europe, Suma Qian in China, and Ibn Khaldun in the Muslim world, all the way to the present. And the more you come to the twentieth century and look at the work of modern historians, the more you find the professionalisation of the field. This meant that historians became more and more focused on trying to be different from everybody else, and establish history as a distinct discipline. The Germans made a very serious attempt to do this, responding to the rise of the Social Sciences. Before that, historians thought they could cover everything of the past, and base their skills largely on their classical training. But many wanted modern history to be more like a science, so they came to focus on archival research. They felt that the use of archival records and first-hand documentation was what distinguished historical science from other fields. Social scientists may work with the more contemporary methodologies that were being developed, for example all kinds of statistical and quantitative data, but historians would concentrate on official archives. This gave the advantage to subjects like diplomatic history, where the records of government-to-government relations were kept. So that focus became very strong. I was trained to do that by historians who were keen on archival research. That was good training which I greatly appreciated. But when I started to teach theory and method myself, I began to realize that, while you can read all the archives you like, there really was too much for any single historian to master and organize into a coherent story without careful selection. And if you have to select and interpret what is selected, you would need a frame in which to ask your questions. You would need some sort of hypothesis to start with because there is just too much out there and you can make little of the archives without one. In other words, you have to start with something, with your premises.

And where do you get your premises from? On what basis do you formulate your premises? In other words, you have to bear in mind the kind of sociology of knowledge behind the premises, how much are you influenced by the dominant ideas and judgments of your own times, by your own personal experiences. How these actually lead you to formulate certain kind of questions. You need to be aware how much the events around you influence the kinds of questions you ask when you look at the past. So that made me much more self-conscious about what we historians were doing and I became dissatisfied with this idea of historians depending mainly on archives without realizing that that's not enough. I learnt a lot from my own students. As we were trying to write Malaysian history, we saw that, if we worked mainly from the archives, we would end up with the British point of view and little else because what we would have done was to pick what the British said about this, that or the other. If you depend on the archives, you could never free yourself of the biases recorded in the official records, the elitist, upper class and bureaucratic interpretation of events. We knew that, for our Malaysian history, that simply was not right. This is also so elsewhere, because if you look at the whole of Southeast Asian studies in general, all the historians of Southeast Asia faced the same problem. They too cannot depend on archives for a fuller understanding of their history. If you do research on Indonesian history and you depend on the Dutch archives, you'll just end up with just one narrow perspective. So Southeast Asian historians could not do what many modern Chinese and Japanese historians tended to do, which was to depend on their archives. The Japanese and Chinese are different because they have large and comprehensive archives of their own which are not foreign-dominated. Southeast Asians (except possibly the Thais) didn't have that. As a result, historians have to turn to other sources, like oral history and other so called secondary sources, and had to acquire new skills to use such secondary sources convincingly. A lot of this meant reading newspapers and magazines of the time, and the analyses of the writings, as well as the memories, of journalists and various other people who had lived through the times. All these sources became more important. It made historians realize that there is a lot to learn from the Social Sciences. How do you control such a wide range of materials? How do you make them valid for your historical work?

VS: *Yes. So this was a radical take on history, this kind of turn to Social Science. Was it resisted? Were there individuals, historians trained in the old school who were uncomfortable with this?*

WGW: Yes, some of my colleagues continued to use the British archives. I'm not criticizing that. That was a job that still needed to be done and we need scholars to do that. If nobody read the archives, there's something wrong with that too. The archives actually provides you with a frame, it's a frame that you can start with. But if you approach it critically, and not accept that frame as a given and work only within that frame, and look at that frame from outside, then having such a frame gives you a start. If you're totally without a frame, that would be like looking at nature where, if there's no frame, and no kind of focus, there could never be a work of art. So this is what the archival frame does. Where archives exist, they help you provide a frame. And every historian should be trained how to deal with archives. The point that I learnt, and all my colleagues learnt to understand, was to train our students to go beyond it. After learning to use the archives, don't just depend on it. As historians, they also have to learn how to control the materials beyond that. I started to read and re-read the work of social scientists, particularly the anthropologists, who seem the closest to us historians.

VS: *Which ones did you read? Do you remember which ones made an impact on you?*

WGW: Well, a bunch of anthropologists were working for the government on Malaysia. On Malaysian aborigines, on Malay society. Some of them were not professional anthropologists but they were working in that framework.

VS: *Colonial administrators?*

WGW: Yes, for example, Raymond Firth, and his wife, on the Malays, Maurice Freedman and Bill Skinner on the Chinese, in Singapore and Thailand respectively. There were others working on the aborigines.

VS: *And you mentioned the sociology of knowledge, so were you like, reading these and other such perspectives?*

WGW: Oh yes. To be fair to my teachers of the colonial era, they introduced that as philosophical background.

VS: *Yes, within the context of history training you mean?*

WGW: I remember reading quite a bit of philosophy. I was already reading Popper and Hayek. When I was an undergraduate, I did economics and was introduced to other parts of Social Science. So I was not entirely innocent. Economists were already pushing us to look at that and when you do economics you do get a sense of the complexities of political economy. Those were very exciting times. And it was not professional sociology or professional social sciences that attracted us. We were reading Karl Marx and, with him, you can't get away from a wide range of social sciences. Before I was trained as a historian, I was reading the Communist Manifesto and whatever we could find of what was considered scientific and progressive at the time, including a few key writings of Lenin and Mao Zedong. These were banned books, but we read them and managed not to get caught.

VS: *Yes. So the training was very inter-disciplinary.*

WGW: That's not training.

VS: *Well, certainly exposure…*

WGW: Yes that's exposure, that's largely through debating amongst ourselves. My generation was an interesting one. I just can't imagine it today. It was after the war and many of my fellow students were older students. I didn't lose too many years because I was able to catch up in school after the war ended, but many others had been ready to go to university in 1941 and therefore lost at least four years. After the war they had to start again and some didn't get to the university until 1947, 1948, or even 1949. So amongst my fellow students were people who had to interrupt their studies, including some who fought in the INA [Indian National Army]. One of them was my roommate in the dormitories. And there were others who were close to people involved in fighting against the Japanese, or in one way or another resisting the Japanese. There was the INA that sided with the Japanese, and the people who were against the Japanese. Amongst the students were people who had been through some harrowing experiences. So when they became undergraduates after the war, they were relatively mature. Thus a lot of our learning was informal, unorthodox and, in many cases, may be described as anti-establishment.

VS: *Would you say the best kind of learning?*

WGW: Oh yes. But anyway, I was not entirely innocent. As students of economics, we were taught the classical work of people like Marshall and his followers and, in particular, the "revisionist" work of Keynes, because that was the time when Keynesian economics was still in the ascendant. So we were familiar with Keynesian economics as a kind of realistic British response to Marx that enabled Britain to avoid revolution. What we learnt about Marx and what Marx was predicting, was met by the ideas of Keynes who, in his way, showed that classical economics could not deal with the problems of liberal capitalism. A completely new kind of economics was needed to solve those problems. There was a need for the judicious use of state power to intervene in the economy in ways that could prevent social disorder and revolution. As students, we were all familiar with that. We argued with our teachers. Some were proponents of classical economics and prone to argue, "Yes, but..." But they encouraged us to read and think more about what these ideas meant for our part of the world.

All that had been set aside when I studied ancient Chinese history for the next few years. But when, after 1959, I turned again to look at modern times and at methodology and theory, much of what I had learnt came back. So it was not too hard for me. I needed to realize that the early informal learning was relevant to the study of history. And I brought that thought into my teaching and to my students. My students were very interested. But of course the subject was still politically sensitive. Even today, there are certain subjects you just don't get into too deeply, particularly with students. Quite frankly, when I was teaching in Kuala Lumpur, and I'm sure this was true in Singapore as well, some university teachers were being watched. I don't know who was watching but I was warned about it. I was warned that Special Branch was looking out for students who would report for them. They paid them a kind of retainer fee, or something like that, to report on what lecturers were saying in class. So I had to be careful. You may think you're being objective but it is chastening to think that you could be seen as something of a threat. I have to say that there were constraints, but I learnt a lot anyway from teaching my students. That was how I opened myself to a lot of other academic disciplines, in fact, to the point of not being too troubled by disciplinary boundaries. And I have been like that ever since. There are historians who ask me, "You still a historian?" I think they have genuine doubts!

VS: *I wanted to bring you back to the present and ask you about your views on China. Much has been made about the, it's sort of a euphemism, a metaphor that one hears in every domain, including the Social Sciences. What is your view about this current euphoria about the rise of China and how it impacts Social Sciences or Social Sciences research?*

WGW: The ramifications are actually quite great. Exactly what the impact would be like years from now, I can't say. For now, I'm not sure it's all euphoria. There's also fear, anxieties about being threatened and mixed feelings of opportunity and risk on the subject. Going back to the question I asked myself when I was young. What went wrong with Chinese society at the turn of the 20th century? What drove so many Chinese intellectuals during the 1920s and 1930s to set aside tradition in order to learn from the West? In 1949, the iconoclasts basically succeeded when the Chinese Communist Party won. They supported a kind of Western heresy, the communist ideals that they took was almost straight from Marx and Engels, Lenin and Stalin. They may have had had their own understanding of what these thinkers predicted, and certainly had reservations about the applicability of some of the goals for China. But they were under the discipline as communist party members. You could say that they still have that power structure and the commitment to party discipline, but at that time, the purpose was to absorb the development goals that the Soviet Union had devised. The Chinese learnt well from that model and some of the leaders were ready to give up their traditional values in order to better ingest key parts of that Western heresy.

But what is so interesting for historians and the other social scientists is to see, whatever you may consciously want to do, that there are developments you can't control or prevent. What happens when someone like Mao Zedong, a very Chinese person who was the product of the Chinese elitist tradition, found that he could not help acting out even that which he professed to reject? At one level, he totally dismissed the Confucian past and talked in the most romantic terms about revolution and class struggle. The language he used was highly inflammatory, stressing the use of violence to destroy the feudal past, and to rid the party off the "new socialist man" that did not meet his standards of revolutionary fervour. At another level in his own thinking, beneath all the slogans, his early educational background came through, and he was still a traditional rebel leader. Even the way he imparted the "socialist" values he took from the West was still Chinese. Like memorizing classical texts, learning was a very holistic process. It's not analytical. The Maoist ideologues claimed that theirs was scientific socialism but what they meant by scientific was essentially to adopt what Lenin and other Marxists had deemed to be scientific. They learnt their doctrines very uncritically, and that itself is a subject of psychological and sociological interest, part of the sociology of knowledge under a specific set of political conditions. This raises questions like how do you structure new kinds of power when you are not really able to shake off older traditions of power? More traditional political culture has survived than most people realize. So when you talk in modern terms, and the language and rhetoric is seemingly modern, but the thinking and the underlying knowledge framework and, in particular, the way new knowledge may be used as a tool of power, as a means of gaining, maintaining, manipulating and controlling, power has much to do with people's deep-rooted political culture. And the people around, and depending on, the power centre are aware of that. There is no escape from this because leaders have to deal with their people, and here we are talking about hundreds of millions of people. How the leaders rule over them, control them and keep them acquiescent, depends on how well they know their psychology. These leaders have to respond to how their people live, what they think is right and wrong, what they understand about authority and accept as legitimate. All these deep-rooted values have nothing to do with Marxism. And this is manifested in the way China has developed during the past three decades. Much of what has happened reminds us how little we can do to shake off the peculiarities of a historical political culture. When that is taken into account, becoming modern is often a misunderstanding if not an illusion. Even when it is real in the conscious mind at a rational moment, it cannot be separated form what is actually there on the ground among the people's shared hopes and desires.

I would say that this is true of India, Southeast Asia and the Islamic world today. The Chinese experience shows that, even when you have gone as far as what Mao

Zedong did in the Cultural Revolution, with his calls for the total negation of the past, calling upon the young people to burn books and symbols of the past and take things out of historic temples and have them destroyed, what happened was that it didn't change the basic values of China's authoritarian traditions. Mao Zedong didn't manage to change himself! Even while he was calling for revolution, he was about as traditionally emperor-like as you could imagine. He didn't seem to realize how he would be seen, because in his own mind, he was the opposite of an emperor. Apart from his appetite for female company, he might even be compared to Mahatma Gandhi if you accept his claims to be someone who lived very simply and was always caring for the welfare of the rural poor. Even though he was ensconced deeply in the former Manchu Qing Imperial Palace, he saw himself as a simple man of the people. So you see how he managed to deceive himself about that. And his self-image was very important. It should have been consistent with his ideology and the rhetoric that he constantly used. But in practice, when it came to manipulating people and using power, arousing people to do what he wanted, he used very traditional ways that were consistent with the political culture operating in that environment.

I think the deep roots of political culture are very important problems for the social sciences. When you look at how people are studying Islam and the strong connection between politics and religion today, perhaps they should also look at China. China is not a particularly religious country and the issue is not the connection with politics, but there are religious and moral values that matter in daily practice. Although they are supposed to have been set aside and marginalized, they are still very much in evidence. These values didn't go away for long or went very far. And it is an important matter to bear in mind when you examine China today, and look at how the young people are learning from the West again. You will see that many of them are learning in a different way. Having set aside one set of Western values received from Russia, they now look at another set that is being received from the United States. It's not Marx anymore, and they seem to have gone much of the way towards Wall Street. That is like going all the way in the opposite direction. But again, the question remains, have they really changed that much? There is evidence that, among some of them, their Chineseness could be as deeply rooted as it ever was. As the young in the cities are now reading the tabloids from Hollywood and New York, or learning everything they can from the latest novels and the latest social science books and journals from the West, they are picking up much that is new. But how deeply does all this go? I think one has to be very cautious in interpreting the changes. When I read the young Chinese scholars today, I find that they can quote any number of the top social scientists in the West, the best economists, political scientists, and sociologists. They can translate their work and quote from these writings extensively. But I wonder how far they actually accept the premises of those social sciences? They look at the methodology, and certainly as pure methodology, and they find no difficulty learning that. Just as in the physical and mathematical sciences, the technical methods can be learnt by anybody. But, as we know, these can be learnt for completely different purposes.

Social science is no different. You learn the methods. You learn economics, the financial calculations, the statistics, but you can use it for different purposes. What you use it for would be rooted in your own continuities, your own past. My understanding is that you can't get away from that. So I really don't know how this fascination with the most up-to-date social science will translate in the long run when the writings are all available in Chinese and widely used by the top people in the field who have often been so well trained in America. If they stay on in America and become Americanized, that's a different story. But if they go back to China and really want to fit into their own society and address their own people, then all they can confidently bring would be the basic methodologies and techniques, but not the underlying premises that the Americans work with.

VS: *In that context, do you think the notion of academic colonialism and Eurocentrism typifies Chinese Social Science today? This sort of turning to the West for...*

WGW: In a way I'm not particularly concerned for the Chinese because they can't escape this stage in their history. They will learn and learn, but they will never go beyond a certain point. Ultimately, we are talking about an ancient civilization. This is not a general experience available to all peoples. It would be different if you didn't have much of a tradition of your own. Then it's much easier to have one new tradition completely take over. For example, if a people have very simple ideas about their lives and you introduce them to a religion that offers them a great deal more than they have ever known, they could be expected to accept the total set of new values and eliminate whatever they had had in the past. That's entirely possible. But I think with the world of politics, economics and modern society, that is unlikely to happen. A well-established civilization would have its own set of traditions and strategies.

VS: *So do you see a kind of indigenous Chinese Social Science emerging?*

WGW: Yes, I think that's what they are talking about.

VS: *Do you see any evidence of it? What is your assessment? Do you think there is a genuine attempt at constructing this?*

WGW: I think there are attempts but it's still early days. Because I think they haven't fully digested what they have learnt, much of the talk is still in the realm of dreams and ambitions. The Chinese are learning the techniques well. But the assumptions underlying the enquiries of social scientists in, say, America, about the way society is or should be organized, how their people generalize their wants and desires, and how prevailing social operations enable people to achieve what they want, these are based on certain ways of doing things that are common in the West, and highly developed and particularised. After the research is done, you come up with certain results, and possibly new theories. But the kind of society from which you drew those results may never have existed in China. So when you bring the methodology to use on a different society, your results may not meet expectations. What do you do then? Do you force the results to conform by making adjustments, tweaking a little here and there so that you can come up with the right conclusions, and also so that your social scientist professors can say, "Oh, good, it works"? Then you're either deceiving your professors or you're deceiving yourself.

Something like that is happening and it is hard to accept the benefits of such research. Others, however, are saying no. They try to use the same or similar techniques taken from the West but ask different questions pertinent to a different cultural framework. That is also happening but there is still uncertainty about the validity of their results because the researchers are themselves not confident of what they are doing without explicit approval of their counterparts abroad. Because the assumptions of a particular methodology, when, where and how the methodology was perfected, can be overwhelming, scholars can't make it work successfully in areas where the underlying premises are different and the questions are worded in a way which is appropriate in one context, but not appropriate in another. The Chinese have been trying very hard with social surveys, for example. They've had at least two decades of experimenting with different kinds of survey methods. Some results are interesting, but no one seems sure they are sound for new theoretical works to emerge because the methodology is derived from different sets of circumstances somewhere else.

VS: *One of the problems that have been noted in Social Science settings outside of Europe and North America is that there has been an unthinking imitation of Western knowledge — including theories and methodologies, and as you say, these don't fit the Asian context. So there is this movement to indigenize the Social Sciences. And I was just wondering if in the Chinese case there is consciousness of this?*

WGW: Oh they definitely are conscious of it. They are in some ways even more conscious about this than scholars in Southeast Asia because they had gone through this strong Marxist phase. Because of that, they had done Marxist theory and method almost to death and now acknowledge that much of it didn't work. So some of them are more wary now and are learning from their mistakes. If all that "scientific" method didn't work, the new theories and methodologies from the United States may also not be adequately domesticated to work in China. So the best social scientists are at least more sensitive to that possibility. There is now a double reluctance, a reluctance that is rooted in their own traditions that makes them more cautious, and the extra reluctance because they have done it once before and then found themselves to be utterly confused by it all. So now that they've come back to look to the West, they would like to avoid applying methodologies that might not work. They do not want to look foolish again and are not happy with some of the younger scholars who go all out to please their American professors and follow exactly what they are taught to do. Others, of course, are concerned to make their careers quickly, and some hope to stay in the United States where they would have to conform to the prevailing standards. But if these scholars go back to China, they know that their contemporaries in China don't accept simple applications of what they had learnt abroad. So they have to adapt and try to modify what they learnt, or turn around to say, "I cannot do the work in China and am going back to work in America". That's the tension that I see. And it'll be like that for quite a while until some genius comes along. You'll need someone like another Marx or Weber, but homegrown in China. India already has produced some social scientists who have done very well. But the Chinese are not quite there yet because they haven't been exposed to Western social science for as long as the Indians have. Some Indians have had five or six generations of people who've been directly absorbing, regurgitating, transforming and internalizing what they have learnt, and then coming up with their own set of theories. China hasn't had that time. Or rather the Chinese did it by following a path that led them astray; they have now doubled back and, in many ways, are starting all over again.

VS: *You've anticipated my next question which is about, okay, well, this is supposed to be the Asian century, with the rise of India and China as economic powers. So do you think this might be the Asian century in terms of intellectual, academic power, whether Chinese, Indian or others?*

WGW: Anything is possible. I mean, a perfect example of someone who's managed to do that is Indian; he is Amartya Sen. China could one day produce somebody of that calibre, but it will take a while; they are not ready for that yet. In the case of India, I mean, I've talked to Amartya, and he talks about his grandfather, his father and the generations of scholars in Bengal! He talks of his grandfather's mixing of great classical knowledge with the understanding of Western philosophy, his father's knowledge of the Sanskrit texts that was imparted to Amartya himself. All that time, there was learning about Western values, but always with a clear understanding as to where it has a place and where it does not. So just to hear Amartya explaining about the three generations and the dimensions of scholarship underlying it all, that's really something!

VS: *Right. Do you see comparable figures in the Chinese context?*

WGW: It's much too early. I don't see anybody like that now. But then I can't say anyone saw someone like Amartya Sen emerging fifty years ago. Tagore was a brilliant example two generations earlier. He was like a flash of lightning. He had no real successors like him, and that was in the field of literature and not the Social Sciences. I don't know what he had to say about the Social Sciences. My friends tell me his poetry is wonderful in Bengali but when he translated his poems, they don't read nearly as well. I've only read some of them in English and have not found them memorable. So even with Tagore, his successes had no bearing on breakthroughs in the social sciences for several decades because the social scientists were not yet ready. It does not have to take that long in China and may happen sooner than that, who knows? After all, developments are faster now. The access to knowledge is much better now, with cyberspace, computers, google and everything, there is just so much more exposure to new data and ideas. It may shorten the time needed for someone to come forth in China. But I expect that it won't be easy.

VS: *Do you think the goal of constructing an indigenous social science is a worthwhile pursuit?*

WGW: I am reminded of an analogy from American history. The American Revolution has been greatly admired — it was anti-colonial, got rid of the British, established the first new nation, and so on. The American Declaration of Independence, drawing from 18th century enlightenment ideals, talks about the 'pursuit of happiness'. I am fascinated by this and believe that the American leaders at the time secretly knew that you could not catch happiness by simply pursuing it. Those who knew that were okay. Those who did not know that are likely in the end to make themselves unhappy. If you run after something rather unpredictable and intangible, you would never catch it. But if you do your best and make progress, you may actually find it one day. As for indigenous social science as an intellectual goal, why not? Go for it, but don't run after it as if it is something real that you can catch. My sense is that if you don't run too hard after it you may actually find it.

This interview is reproduced with kind permission of the International Sociological Association.

Rethinking Chinese History in a Global Age: An Interview with Wang Gungwu

by Alan Baumler

The Chinese Historical Review 14, no. 1
(Spring 2007): 97–113

Alan Baumler (AB): *To what extent have your personal experiences shaped the type of questions you ask and the type of history you do? What changes do you anticipate (or see) in the next generation of historians given their different experiences and interests?*

Wang Gungwu (WGW): I have been deeply influenced by my personal experiences. My formal education began at a school in the British Malay States during the 1930s and we were given a dose of "British imperial and commonwealth history". Some of the accounts of heroic British adventurers who defeated the Spanish and the French were interesting and taught me a lot about world geography, especially about the American and African continents. British failures in North America that lost them the Thirteen Colonies were touched on more lightly but were very intriguing. It led me later to read American revolutionary and civil war history with particular interest. East of Suez, however, the text focused attention on India and the British colonies in Australia and New Zealand.

As a Chinese boy who was being introduced to many aspects of ancient Chinese history at home by my parents, my formal and informal historical worlds never met. So there was no collusion between the two. Both the British and the Chinese in Malaya at the time did not want to excite our young minds with too many details about earlier Anglo-Chinese conflicts. There was enough nationalistic rhetoric around among the Chinese, and the British were happy to leave the emotional outbursts to be directed against the Japanese invading China. In any case, my history teacher in school was dull and perfunctory while my father's strong love of early Chinese literature and history was infectious. There was really no contest. I was bitten by the stories drawn from the Spring and Autumn Annals (Zuoshi chunqiu 左氏春秋) and Sima Qian's Records of History (司马迁，史记) and other tales of courage and talent that were meant to attract the young to admire a splendid civilization. I sometimes wonder what might have been had my education been more balanced, for example, if the British had concentrated on the great classical stories from Greece and Rome that they taught the children of their own elites rather than on what their sailors, soldiers and merchants did to expand their empire. Later in my studies at university, I did find the ancient world of the Fertile Crescent and the Mediterranean fascinating but, by that time, I was leaning towards the study of Chinese history.

These memories and my subsequent choices of research topics lead me to believe that historians are influenced by personal experiences, although not all of them as directly as my own. Therefore, I tend to assume (and this is obviously not always justified) that my students are not that different from me in this respect and that future generations in Asia will ask quite different questions from those I had asked over the years. They will reflect their own experiences of an even more globalized world, their greater hopes for an "Asian renaissance" and the self-confidence and dignity that preceding generations did not have. I have no doubt these will shape the ways they think about the past and guide them to re-interrupt that past in the history they will eventually write.

AB: *May we ask you to describe for us the key transformations or stages in the evolution of your very influential and versatile academic career? What has motivated you to make important decisions in your research? In other words, how you decide what is important to write about and how you write about the important topics?*

WGW: The first decisions were made for me. My colonial school was shut down when the Japanese occupied Malaya from 1941 till 1945. I stayed home to live in my parents' Chinese world, one that became more important for me because they did not allow me to go to a Japanese school during the occupation years. When the British returned after 1945 to resume teaching "imperial and commonwealth history", the subject had totally lost appeal. Instead, I prepared to return to China in 1947 to attend my father's university in Nanjing to study literature. A year and a half later, at the very end of 1948, when the People's Liberation Army was arriving on the banks of the Yangzi, the National Central University closed down and I was soon back in what had by then become the Federation of Malaya in the midst of a Communist insurgency. At the new University of Malaya that I then joined in 1949, the history courses were broader. In addition to ancient history, we turned to modern Asia in the context of "Asia and Western Dominance". This was incidentally the title of the book by K.M. Pannikar published in 1953. The sub-title said it all: *A Survey of the Vasco da Gama Epoch of Asian History, 1498–1945*. My Chinese background made me skeptical of such an "epoch", but I was persuaded that modern history began in the West with the Italian Renaissance and the expeditions of Columbus in search of a new route to China and India across the Atlantic.

1953 was actually the year after I had decided to train to be an historian. I started with modern history but it soon became clear that I could not study China because China was communist and the governments of Malaya and Singapore were fiercely anti-communist and suspected every Chinese of communist sympathies. All books published in Chinese were carefully examined and no books published in Chinese about modern China were allowed. Having decided I wanted to study China, I went back to what my father had taught me of the ancient historical classics. Hence my first work, *The Nanhai Trade*. This was an early history of Chinese trade in the South China Sea that took me from ancient times to the end of the Five Dynasties (907–960). From 1953 till I completed my doctoral research at the School of Oriental and African Studies in 1957, I immersed myself in the first 1,200 years of imperial history. They were exhilarating years, so much to learn and so few people to learn from or learn with, both in Malaya and in Britain. My second work, the political history of the late Tang and Wudai periods, was completed in 1957 and later published as

The Structure of Power in North China during the Five Dynasties.

The next change came on my return to teach at the University of Malaya (1957–1968). Malaya became independent in 1957 and teaching Chinese history was not enough. I was once again drawn to modern history by the new national consciousness in Asia, especially to post-colonial Southeast Asian history and the challenge of identity reorientation that the Chinese in the region all had to face. On the one hand were the growing pains of the local nationalist intelligentsia; on the other the specter of every Chinese being tarred as potential "fifth column" communists. I still hoped to continue to finish my remaining work on the Song reunification (960–1276) but also decided to begin studying the origins of Chinese settlements in Southeast Asia by going back to the beginning of the Ming dynasty (1368–1644). I stayed in the Song and the Ming periods as long as I could, but my teaching duties and the pressure of events affecting the overseas Chinese drew me to modern and contemporary affairs.

You can see how often events had influenced the direction of my research and forced me to learn about things that I had not planned to study. At the same time, they had also allowed me to return to my original interest in modern history by a rather roundabout route. I am grateful for all that because they enabled me to learn about the modern imperial West, thrust me towards the study of ancient Chinese political culture and then brought me back to the Asia that the West had remoulded for at least 200 years. But I have to confess that many of the topics

I wrote about were important to me at the time of writing rather than because I thought they were that important in themselves.

AB: *What advice do you have for the Chinese historians who came to the West to study and are now teaching outside China?*

WGW: I am not sure how my experiences can be relevant for others. I began studying reform and revolution (focusing on Kang Youwei and Sun Yat-sen) because I wanted to understand why they had despaired of the old China, what they expected China to change into, and why Chinese civilization failed to match that of the West. I have never lost interest in these questions. But I was diverted from things modern for more than a decade, so I set out to learn new fields and ask different questions of China's past. One thing I can say is that looking out for research topics that could help you to understand the conditions of your times was exciting in itself. You get to learn so much more besides what you intended to spend years researching on. Had my life not been so touched by the political events in China and Southeast Asia during the 15 years from the late 1930s, I might not have studied history at all but gone to Europe to study what would look today like post-imperial cultural studies. My early interest in languages and literatures was largely past-oriented, but it need not have led me to the profession of history.

One other point: my undergraduate training had little to do with China, my teaching at the University of Malaya (1957–1968) was increasingly about Southeast Asian and

European institutions and ideas, and my later research included the Chinese abroad and China's relations with its neighbors. But all that time, I continued to read and study all I could about the history of China itself. There was so much to learn but I was encouraged to believe that everything I learnt was not only related but also helped me to learn other things. Most of all, I discovered that whenever I had to teach a new subject or to connect what I know to what my students and colleagues wanted to know, that was another opportunity to learn more history to help me in my profession.

AB: *In your view, what are the major differences between the way historical scholarship is done in various places?*

WGW: My generation was trained to use the archives but, unlike our teachers who had used those in Portugal, Spain, France and the Netherlands, we were familiar only with British documents in Singapore and in London. For someone who wanted to work on China, the Chinese archives were not available to us at the time. By turning to pre-modern Chinese history, one had to be content with Chinese published documents. Then language, literary, philosophical, and philological and even some epigraphic skills were needed for close textual examinations. This led the historian back to classical studies and a background in the humanities as distinct from the social sciences. For this, one would need some formal training in *Hanxue* 汉学, what the Europeans call Sinology.

　　For students in modern history, it is now no longer enough to depend on the archives; quantitative and statistical skills, so-called "secondary" sources, including oral history, are all invaluable. The modern/pre-modern divide was once difficult to bridge in Asia. It is easier today and we see more history centers demanding familiarity with a wide range of humanities and social science skills from their students. This is more true in Southeast Asia than in China and other Northeast Asia countries where historians are normally strongly grounded in the whole length of their history and historians are expected to begin with a mastery of each country's ancient history. Given my experiences, I think that this way provides the future historian with a deeper sense of what is possible in the history profession.

AB: *As someone who has been doing a lot of cross-cultural, cross-region scholarship, what is your view on the future trends of historical scholarship? There has been a lot of talk in the United States about internationalization of American history, that is, to emphasize the connections between what happened domestically and internationally and to get rid of the traditional paradigm of American exceptionalism. Any thought on this question?*

WGW: National histories are recent phenomena. My experience doing research in pre-modern history has shown that cross-border, cross-region and even cross-cultural scholarship was the norm almost everywhere until the 19th century. The rise in national historiography coincided with the rise of the United States. Thus, the exceptional nation-building and continental-expansion experience gave US historians much to do to explain the country's extraordinary success. That kind of exceptionalism is understandable. Actually the more challenging question is whether, when American historians internationalize their history, especially those with strong social science aspirations, they would move from exceptionalism to claims for universalism. That leads to the well-intentioned but presumptuous path when they expect other countries and regions to be ultimately more like America and the scholars elsewhere to think and behave like those in America. It would be a pity if scholarly research is diverted to making this happen and scholars are concerned to find out when and where this might or might not happen, and why and why not. Nevertheless, I do favour what you call "internationalization" because I see that as the historical norm and expect our nation-centered historiography to become less narrowly focused and openly recognize the past global linkages of our various regions more readily.

AB: *Much historical scholarship has been created in response to the needs of colonial and national states. To what extent to you think that demand for popular history, in whatever form, is or will effect the production of history in Asia?*

WGW: It is fascinating to see how readily young Asian scholars have taken to popular histories in many of its forms. This is particularly true in South and Southeast Asian history because their historiographical traditions have not been bureaucratic, politicized or overwhelming as they were in Northeast Asia. Even in China, the trend away from orthodox political and economic history is beginning to show, partly because the younger generation are increasingly distrustful of government-sponsored writings and keen to find alternative histories to challenge received wisdom. If this trend continues, and it is unlikely that states will openly disallow it, it will change the balance of history writing in Asia. I am particularly struck by the number of studies on labor and gender histories, on the history of popular culture, the media and popular arts, and on the history of the environment being published in several Asian countries in recent years.

AB: *You are one of the few scholars who have done work on both modern and pre-modern state-building. The contrasts between building a state during the Five Dynasties and building modern Malaysia are obviously huge. Do you see any important commonalities or points of comparison between modern and pre-modern state-building?*

WGW: Yes, the differences are great. It would be stretching it to find anything that could be clearly described as commonalities. There are simply too many distinct variables between North China and a post-colonial multi-cultural state like Malaysia. One could make one or two useful comparisons: for example, the role of the families that produced key members of the bureaucracy and the ways they prevented the state from being dominated by the military. The descendants of residual Tang functionaries helped to stabilize the dynasties of the 10th century when given the chance to do so. In Malaysia, it was those who worked under British tutelage who produced or trained the new generations of bureaucrats.

Another example is to note how Tang Administrative Law preserved after the dynasty had fallen continued to play a part in keeping the rival warlords within the range of successful administrative practices. Similarly, the retention of British ideals about the rule of law provided a major support for the efforts to keep disparate communal interests committed to the new nation-state. The major contrast, however, was in the different primary foundations of legitimate power. In North China, the strength of the military was crucial while, in Malaysia, that power rested in a modern political coalition party that made consensus-building the basis of national unity.

Within a single country, commonalities between pre-modern and modern state building can more easily be found. In China, we could say that both the modern and pre-modern state depended on military victory to establish legitimacy. Placing the emperor (today the Communist Party) above the law, and then turning to a mandarinate that was at base Confucian (today the current set of technocrats who are key party cadres) in order to consolidate control. From the anarchic conditions at the end of the Tang dynasty (late 9th century), a mixed Toba-Turk and Han military elite took more than eighty years to fight off external enemies while struggling to win local "civil wars". In the 20th century, following the break-up of the imperial system and its replacement by an untried republican constitution, sovietized and nationalist Chinese took over sixty years to neutralize their external enemies sufficiently. Only then could the winning side in the civil war proclaim that the new People's Republic of China had "stood up".

AB: *Much of your work has involved Chinese sojourners, people of Chinese descent living outside China but planning to return at some point and their complex relationships with China and Chinese-ness. To what extent and in what ways do you think "China" is relevant to the current trans-national economic and cultural networks of the "Overseas Chinese."*

WGW: In the past, the sojourning Chinese internalised their sense of "China" and promised to rejoin their families in various villages and towns, each in their minds a sort of microcosm of "China". When imperial China was keen on foreign trade, it did little to help them abroad, but with both the Ming and Qing dynasties (until 1893), the Chinese who ventured overseas were treated with suspicion and they were often actually punished when they returned. On the other hand, a poor and disunited China, especially in the first half of the 20th century, sought their help, rekindled their confidence, and appealed to their patriotism. Now that China is doing well economically and actively wielding influence abroad, the Chinese market is certainly relevant to a spectrum of various kinds of Chinese networks. But there is a big difference between the *huayi* (those of Chinese descent, 华裔) of Southeast Asia at one extreme and the bulk of the new migrants in the West at the opposite end. The former have made their homes outside China for generations (their homes today could be in several countries) and are unlikely ever to wish to be involved in China's internal or external politics. The latter could still be drawn in, especially if they live in stable and confident liberal democracies like North America and

Australasia that permit their participation in homeland politics. In between, there are many groups that are not comfortable to be too closely tied to China but prefer to leave their options open. Those involved in business with China would, of course, always value their business and professional access to China from outside.

AB: *In Anglo-Chinese Encounters you quote Arthur Waley who suggests that the British encounter with China was first controlled by men who went to Asia "to convert, trade, rule or fight" and only later by those who came "simply to make friends and learn." The British imperial project was then largely taken over by the Americans. To what extent is the rising influence of China in Asia a continuation of these imperial trends and to what extent do you see this as different?*

WGW: If you mean will the rising influence of China in Asia resemble the Anglo-American project, I would say it is different. Apart perhaps from the Qin-Han period of about two centuries (3rd–1st centuries BC), China never had the overwhelming military power that the US has today or what the British had earlier, and, even then, at its peak 2,000 years ago, Chinese power was awesome only in the eyes of its immediate neighbors. After that, the Chinese dynastic rulers (excluding the Mongol Yuan) never sought to convert, rule, or fight outside what they considered their natural borders and, from 1368 till the 20th century, hardly encouraged their merchants to trade abroad. The second Ming emperor sent Zheng He's expeditions to show off his maritime power and then stopped it altogether. The

Manchu Qing who conquered the Ming empire from outside the Great Wall went on to expand westwards to Xinjiang because their partnership with the Mongols led them to think of the steppes and the Tibetan highlands as their own natural border region. In short, I don't see China today ever rising to the kind of Anglo-American dominance that has characterized the past two centuries.

I think Arthur Waley was over-simplifying when he described later Britons as going to China "simply to make friends and learn". Some certainly did that and so did some Americans after 1945 and they made many friends. But, on the whole, with the British, the urge to trade and rule was very strong and, with the Americans, the stronger urge was to trade and convert. Neither thought much about learning, least of all from China. Today, the Chinese official agenda for the country is to make friends wherever it can and also to learn how to develop into a rich and strong country from Great Powers with scientific and technological superiority.

AB: *Your work has often centered on issues of identity, often political identity and especially national identity. You have also looked at the roles of ethnic Chinese economic networks. Do you think there is important work to be done on religious and social networks?*

WGW: Yes, there is much to be done on the social and religious life of the Chinese communities themselves. When I started researching on the subject, issues of nationality and political loyalty were especially important and urgent and I was interested to find out the historical background to the Chinese idea of "identity", how broad or narrow it was, how fluid or unchangeable, who decided what it comprised and how much room did the Chinese overseas have to choose their identity if they wanted a change. And, of course, I was led to consider the relationship between trading networks and political authorities and how multiple identities were managed. Other historians worked on social and religious networks, but these were often more diffused and the sources about them were harder to come by. Official documents were fewer and the researchers had to do a great deal of fieldwork and rely on private sources, interviews and surveys. In some countries in Southeast Asia where there had been communal conflicts, this kind of work was highly restricted, if not prohibited, because of religious and other ethnic/cultural sensitivities. On the whole, the situation is better today and much more work can be done. These are areas where I think valuable contributions can be made and I would like to see more scholars explore questions pertaining to the ups and downs of religious revivalism in modern history. For this-worldly Chinese who live in increasingly Christian, Muslim or Buddhist societies, this is becoming a special challenge. How they had dealt with such phenomena in the past may help us understand what they and the authorities today have to do to handle such problems without fear of social disorder.

AB: *You have stated that you are uncomfortable with the term Chinese Diaspora, especially when it leads to too direct comparisons to the Jewish Diaspora. Do you think that the comparison to the Indian Diaspora works better?*

Has the experience of the Indians overseas been different primarily because of their closer connection to a single empire and the different history of Indian nationalism?

WGW: Yes, the comparison with the Indian diaspora works better in some respects but even there, the difference is significant. There has not been for India until very recently the kind of direct official involvement in diaspora affairs that characterized modern Chinese governments. As long as the imperial dynasties did not care about them, the Chinese overseas learnt to fend for themselves and many individuals had to pay a high price for that. Unfortunately, direct political interventions by Chinese authorities gave the impression that whole Chinese communities were patriotic and loyal only to China and their presence in Southeast Asia was a prelude to China's dominance one day. In the context of the Cold War and fears of communism, a strong centralized power that supported its diaspora and counted on its loyalty made the position of most Chinese overseas exceedingly delicate. The nature of a Chinese nationalism that traced its origins to overseas Chinese communities and other external connections also contributed to this precarious situation. In contrast, the Indian nationalism directed towards Britain was relatively mild. Much greater energies were focused on making the diverse and complex peoples of India grow the sense of nationhood and little attention was paid to the diaspora.

Many other factors lie behind the difference between Indian and Chinese attitudes about trading overseas. The Indians started earlier than the Chinese in Southeast Asia and had considerable impact on the religious and political institutions of that region. But they pulled back and were replaced by Muslims from Iran and the Arab world. Then came the Chinese and even fewer Indians traded abroad. It was not until well after the spread of the British Empire to the east that their numbers began once again to increase. By that time, the Chinese had learnt to work with different local polities and also with the Europeans who began to dominate the region from the 17th century onwards. Thus, at no time were the Chinese dependent on any single power centre while they built their essentially private merchant networks. In contrast, most Indians in the second half of the 19th and the first half of the 20th centuries traded and worked abroad to meet British needs and it was the special British imperial connection that explains much of the global distribution of Indians today.

AB: *In your recent works, you focus on globalization and its ramifications, especially migrating populations. How would you compare the peopling of the New World around 16th–17th century and the current migrations around the world? How would you compare either of these to the movement of Chinese to Southeast Asia?*

WGW: I am not sure there can be comparisons across the board. The peopling of the New World includes the coming of conquerors, colonists, missionaries who had the power to bring or admit later arrivals to work for them. The category of "colonists" was distinctive and so was the lack of national boundaries in the Americas. Their capacity to negotiate with and ultimately push back indigenous peoples and acquire large swathes of land was unique.

That opportunity will not come again and certainly not something that the current migration populations expect. One can find some general similarities that all migrants experience, whether in the 16th–17th century or today, but they are not significant.

The Chinese movement to Southeast Asia that peaked in the late 19th and early 20th century was peculiar to the period and resembles neither the New World of the 16th–17th century nor the current migrations. Before that peak period and perhaps among migrants since the end of the Second World War, Chinese merchants and contract workers did move in ways that are comparable to that of entrepreneurial networks in practice today. But the comparisons are unlikely to yield any significant new information about migrations histories. My view, in any case, is that the differences among all these different waves of migrations are far more interesting than the similarities.

AB: *The study of the Chinese who left China has gone from a minor scholarly byway to a major field of study in the last forty years in part because of economic and political changes have led to increased interest in these topics and thus increased funding. Do you think there are any topics that are currently not receiving the attention they deserve because they do not fit in with contemporary concerns?*

WGW: I am impressed by the remarkable growth of "diasporic" studies pertaining to the Chinese in North America and Australasia during the past two decades. The availability of archival sources and the lack of restrictions

on what might be "sensitive" subjects in these two
regions have been the major reasons why the field has
expanded so quickly. This is simply not so in Southeast
Asia. Funding for research is still limited there and most
scholars find it prudent to avoid subjects of this kind that
attract official attention. As a result, the field is far from
growing. Everything, of course, is relative. The situation
was much worse in the 1960s and that lasted at least
two decades. A small recovery of interest began in the
1990s and some progress can be found in Singapore and
Malaysia, but very little elsewhere. In Indonesia, dramatic
changes have recently been observed but only because
there were such strict taboos on the subject during the
Suharto years (1966–1998) that any glimmer of light has
been greeted with acclamation. In short, there are vast
areas that await qualified researchers, but they can be
tackled only by the intrepid and the determined in the
face of suspicious political cultures hardened by decades
of prejudice against either Chinese wealth-making or
Chinese radical ideologies. The numerous and ingenious
ways that Chinese communities have adapted to local
conditions over the past century — not only in economic
and political spheres, but also in their social, religious, and
cultural ways of life — and the impact they have had on
the new nation-states and the emerging middle classes in
each of them deserves urgent attention. If these subjects
had been allowed to receive the kind of attention that the
Chinese Americans have received in the last dozen years,
they would have led scholars to fill many shelves in our
university libraries.

AB: *In Earthbound China you take up the theme of the "Continental mind-set" and the idea of maritime China as a minor tradition. Recent work by F.W. Mote and others has emphasized the complex interplay between the cultural and political systems of the central plain and those of the non-Han peoples. How do you think the history of 19th and 20th century China would look different if scholars really did take up Sun Yat-sens dictum that the "huaqiao is the mother of revolution?"*

WGW: Fritz Mote and others are quite right to emphasize the complex interplay of systems within China throughout history. This was part of the continental mindset I stressed in my book. The distinctions drawn along the China coasts were much simpler. People coming by sea were either friendly traders or unfriendly raiders (including pirates and smugglers). Eventually, no Chinese could trade abroad privately. Therefore, no political or cultural systems were involved and interactions were kept to a minimum. Hence the lack of preparedness when the Europeans arrived by sea in the 16th century and the great surprise when the British fleets defeated the Chinese so decisively in the middle of the 19th century. Nevertheless, maritime China was a minor tradition because the Chinese navy was strong between the Song and the Ming dynasties (from the 11th to the 15th century) and hundreds of thousands of coastal Chinese were engaged in seagoing activities for a thousand years before modern times. What prevented that tradition from growing stronger was a question of imperial policies determined by historical concerns with overland defense against China's most dangerous enemies. That began to change since the 19th century and current policy suggests that the Chinese are determined never to allow its maritime defenses to be weak again.

I am not sure what exactly you have in mind about Sun Yat-sen's dictum and 19th & 20th century Chinese history. The "mother of revolution" slogan reflected the help Sun personally received when he was in exile with a price on his head and, to the extent that he personified the revolution, the slogan was more than words. Many pro-Guomindang *huaqiao* in Southeast Asia and North America did take it seriously, and this was reflected largely in scholarship of the Republican period. But none of the published writings have impinged on mainstream republican historiography. Your question may be one of those "if" questions that would not take us very far.

AB: *In much of your work you emphasize the importance of the Japanese invasion in creating nationalism in Southeast Asia. This has also been an important recent trend in China studies. What do you think are the most helpful insights scholars of China could borrow from the literature on Southeast Asia?*

WGW: Yes, the Japanese were important in inspiring nationalism against Western colonialism in Southeast Asia, notably after they defeated the Russians in 1905. Many Southeast Asian scholars also believe that the Japanese invasions of 1941–1945 speeded up the decolonization process in Southeast Asia. I am not, however, sure how much their writings are relevant to Chinese scholars who work on Sino-Japanese relations. The inspiration that

Japan's modernization offered to China at the turn of the 20th century was soon replaced by growing distrust following Japan's demands in Manchuria after defeating the Russians, the Japanese takeover of Korea and finally the Twenty-One Demands of 1915. Chinese scholars have then underlined the further encroachments on Chinese soil during the next two decades that did so much to create a new and much deeper nationalism that had Japan as the target. Their writings show that the several Japanese pushes into China beginning in Manchuria in 1931 gave Chinese nationalism its particular stridence, and that the war of 1937–1945 still provides the trigger, if not the core, of contemporary Chinese nationalism. In comparison, it is striking that the older nationalism aroused by the Great Powers, against the British and French, then Russians and Germans at other times, are now described rather perfunctorily. Even the nationalism against the Americans of the 1947–54 years that seemed to have aroused so much emotion at the time seems lightly touched on without emphasis. In all these cases, the record of past grievance is mentioned and explained as something regrettable but past. Only where the Japanese invasion is concerned are feelings still described in strong language.

The resentments are traced back a long way, from at least the Twenty-One Demands and the Versailles Treaty — the start of the May Fourth Movement — to the unending Japanese pressure to take Chinese lands after the end of the age of High Imperialism, after other Great Powers had stopped doing so in Asia. As for the years from the 1930s to 1945, the books are replete with details of the killings, tortures and humiliations at the hands of the

Japanese, most notably the "Rape of Nanking". In short, anti-Japanese nationalism hardened over a period of some thirty years as contrasted with the three and a half years of Japanese Occupation of the Southeast Asian region. So it would not occur to Chinese historians to compare their nationalism with those of the Southeast Asians. In addition, the Japanese preached liberation from Western imperialism to the elites of Southeast Asia and encouraged their nationalism against the Western colonial powers. Only the overseas Chinese were singled out for harsh treatment wherever there were large Chinese communities, notably Singapore, the various states of Malaysia and some parts of Indonesia and the Philippines. Thus, although Southeast Asian historians record the hard times of the occupation period, there was no reason for prolonged bitterness among the indigenous nationalists as among the Chinese. Unlike for the Chinese, it was easier for them to forget, and even forgive, when the Japanese offered compensation and apologized for any wrongdoing.

Chinese historians have noted that Southeast Asian writings about their anti-colonial nationalisms vary from the relative lack of bitterness in countries like Malaysia and the Philippines to the more systematic criticisms in Vietnam, Myanmar and Indonesia. Compared to the Chinese attitudes towards the European powers that had humiliated them, the differences are not so great. Criticisms of the Europeans in the history textbooks are not accompanied by deep feelings of resentment. The contrast is clearer, however, when Chinese point to the depth of feelings among the Koreans towards their Japanese colonial rulers. Such comparisons tend to re-enforce Chinese nationalism against

Japanese militarism as well as against those in Japan today who are proud of their wartime behavior in China.

AB: *In "The University as a Global Institution" you discuss the issue of academic freedom and mention that you "have yet to meet a teacher or student in China who did not believe that the academic freedom that would permit the free exchange of knowledge." I was wondering how you see this aspiration towards a university as a place of intellectual exchange in relation to competing visions of the university as training places for national elites, engines of economic growth, or preservers of national or regional traditions.*

WGW: Those who believe in academic freedom don't think there are any contradictions among the competing visions that you mention. Short-term training of specific skills may require carefully packaged courses that leave no time for intellectual exchange, and states that are in a hurry to train such people may well be impatient with demands for freedoms that do not contribute directly to producing the personnel they urgently want. But the teachers or trainers themselves need to be more than mere transmitters of packaged knowledge. They need to understand what they are teaching and the conditions under which the new knowledge they are imparting has been acquired. Their higher levels of education would have to be open to the kinds of free exchange that enhances understanding and adds value to their ability to motivate and inspire their students to be leaders and genuine elites and more efficient engines of economic growth. Even for those who would be the preservers of traditions, free exchange is more likely to help them distinguish the living and dynamic from the moribund and dying aspects of their traditions.

All the scholars I met in China who have made contributions in their respective fields have confirmed their belief in the free exchange of knowledge for them and their students and colleagues. This would not only include their right to disagree with official accounts and explanations that are contrary to reason and the facts but also to allow regular exchanges with foreign or foreign-based Chinese scholars and eventually the employment of such scholars in order to enrich each university's knowledge base. This impression I have is one that was first formed in the 1980s when most scholars were tentative but hopeful. Since the early 1990s, however, the scholars have been increasingly confident about the efficacy of the ideal and the possibility that it is something that will take root at least within the major campuses.

AB: *I was also wondering if a single purpose for a university is even realistic for large universities like NUS, Beida (Beijing or Peking University), or Michigan. In Bind Us in Time you refer to examples of fairly small institutions like the missionary colleges that could have a unitary vision, or larger institutions like the University of Chicago, which maintain such a vision only through considerable effort.*

WGW: The universities in China are undergoing changes at a rapid pace. Not all the changes are necessarily for the better and some experiments are clearly unsuccessful when administrators and academics use them for contrary purposes.

Among those I would consider wasteful and unlikely to deliver is the mad rush to make every kind of college some kind of university and then try to reproduce the missions that the great universities of the world set for themselves. The desire to do well is commendable and the Chinese universities today do aim very high. But for the past five years, there has been an over-supply of graduates coming onto the job market without the skills the country most needs. It may take some time for optimistic and entrepreneurial educationists to be realistic about what it takes to reach the high standards they want. What is regrettable is the waste of scarce resources while they are learning.

The level of debate among those who genuinely want their universities to achieve international recognition, however, is encouraging. It is sometimes surprising how badly they want it and how high a price they are prepared to pay to attain that recognition. Re-appraisals have already begun and resources are being rationalized. This may seem easier to do if some strong central directions are given, but that would also be contrary to the spirit of decentralization that has enabled much of the country's development to have taken place at such breakneck speed. Personally, I sympathize with the need to nurse educational resources with great care. But I am also concerned not to see the heavy hand of central bureaucracies take away the right of scholars to have more input into the direction of university and college development. There seems to me no alternative to local experiments that allow academics to make advances through trial and error while they are being open to learning from comparable lessons elsewhere.

AB: *In one of your lectures on Chinese identity, you mentioned that the term Chinese is overworked, meaning, it has been overused to describe things/people who have otherwise completely different identities. This is perhaps more true than ever as such a large volume of people of Chinese descent scattering outside the mainland, in Hong Kong, Taiwan, Macau, Southeast Asia and other parts of the world. The problem is that these so-called "Chinese" do not really communicate with each other as "fellow compatriots." Their identities lie somewhere else. How useful is the cultural or ethnic identity in this highly globalized world? Would a successful "Rise of China" help strengthening the Chinese identity and reconnecting the Chinese around the world?*

WGW: This will always be a difficult issue. The many paradoxes of globalization apply here to the question of local, ethnic, racial and national identities. My original discussion about the word "Chinese" came from my frustration with the fact that, unlike in the Chinese language itself, there is only one word in most foreign languages for everything to do with the civilization, the empire, the country, the language, the peoples, the traditions and the artifacts that are in any way associated with that large block of land known as "China". To me, the idea of "China" is more like that of "Europe"; it is problematical to equate it with a nation-state or an ethnic group. The closest equivalent in the Chinese language is the word *hua* (flower, beautiful,

华) and that is more accurately used for the people who share the same *hua* or *zhonghua* (middle flower, 中华) civilization, something broad and vague enough to have many layers of meaning.[1] Thus it is not easily compared with more specifically limited ethnicities like the Tibetan or the Mongol or smaller groups like the Yao or the Wa or, outside China, like the Javanese or the Minangkabau or, for that matter, like the Belgian and the Dane in Europe. If "European" is too broad, one might compare "Chinese" perhaps to the "Anglo-Saxon" or "Anglo-Celt" or "German" or "Latino", all words that need to be contextualized. Another set of comparable portmanteau names in common usage would be the Arab, the Indian, the African, the Turk and the Slav. If such comparisons are made, obviously the word "Chinese" will always need qualification as is also needed by each of the other words. But does that matter to the people themselves? As long as "Chinese" is not used merely for a nationality or citizenry, the word could be as useful as the people who so identify want it to be, or as useful as others who want to point to them would want it for.

In short, ethnicity is more about self-identification than about law or politics. Strict definitions are more matters of concern to social science scholars and census takers than to the people who call themselves, or are called, by any "ethnic" label. In fact, when the numbers involved are so large and so closely identified with a historic civilization and a potentially powerful country, the term will remain useful and likely to be kept alongside other identities — to be taken out for display when appropriate and beneficial and to be left unmentioned when it is either unnecessary or inconvenient to do so. Depending on circumstances, a successful China could help reconnect some "Chinese" with other "Chinese" but only if doing so is acceptable in the global/regional context of time and place at the moment of self-identification. If answering to being Chinese is not illegal, nor immoral, it would become attractive for those who can do so to make their private identity public and strengthen their claim to Chinesseness.

Note

1. In ancient Chinese, the two words, 华 (flowery, beautiful) and 花 (flower) were interchangeable in ancient Chinese, thus "flowery" carries the meaning of "splendid" and "beautiful."

This interview is reproduced with kind permission of *The Chinese Historical Review*.

Professor Wang Gungwu Curriculum Vitae

National University of Singapore University Professor, and Emeritus Professor of The Australian National University, Canberra.

Born in Surabaya, Indonesia on October 9, 1930. Australian Citizen.

Educated at Anderson School, Ipoh, Malaysia 1936–46

National Central University, Nanking, China 1947–48

University of Malaya, Singapore 1949–54 (B.A. General 1952; B.A. Honours in History, Upper Second 1953; M.A. 1955)

University of London, School of Oriental and African Studies 1954–57 (Ph.D. 1957)

Taught at University of Malaya, Singapore: Assistant Lecturer 1957–59; Lecturer 1959

University of Malaya, Kuala Lumpur: Lecturer 1959–61; Senior Lecturer 1961–63

Dean of the Faculty of Arts 1962–63; Professor of History 1963–68

Australian National University: Professor of Far Eastern History 1968–1986

Head of Department, 1968–1975, 1980–1986; Director, Research School of Pacific Studies, 1975–1980; Emeritus Professor since 1988

Visiting Appointments, 1961–1983:

1961–62, University of London, Rockefeller Fellow

1972, University of London, Senior Visiting Fellow.

1974–75, All Souls College, Oxford University, Visiting Fellow.

1981, University of Hawaii, John A. Burns Distinguished Professor of History.

1982, National University of Singapore, Visiting Professor.

1983, University of Kansas, Rose Morgan Professor of History.

Vice-Chancellor (President), The University of Hong Kong, 1986–1995.

Chairman, Institute of East Asian Political Economy, Singapore, 1996–1997.

Distinguished Professorial Fellow, Institute of Southeast Asian Studies, Singapore, 1996–2002.

Director, East Asian Institute and Faculty Professor in the Faculty of Arts and Social Sciences, NUS, 1997–2007

National University of Singapore University Professor since 2007

Awards

Fellow of the Australian Academy of the Humanities 1971 (President of the Academy 1980–1983)

Member, Academia Sinica 1992

Foreign Honorary Member, American Academy of Arts and Science 1994

Honorary Member, Chinese Academy of Social Sciences 1996

Commander of the British Empire 1991

International Academic Prize, Fukuoka Asian Cultural Prizes 1994

Honorary D.Litt.: The University of Sydney 1991; The University of Hull 1998

The University of Hong Kong 2002; Open University of Hong Kong 2007

University of Cambridge 2009

Honorary LL.D.: Monash University, Melbourne 1993; The Australian National University 1996; The University of Melbourne 1997

Honorary D.Univ.: Soka University, Tokyo 1990; Griffith University, Brisbane 1994

Honorary Fellow, School of Oriental and African Studies, London 1996

Honorary Professor: University of Hong Kong 1991; Fudan University, Shanghai 1995

Peking University, Beijing 1995; Jinan University, Guangzhou 1998

Nanjing University, Nanjing 2001; Tsinghua University, Beijing, 2004

Xi'an Jiaotong University, 2006

Distinguished Service Award, National University of Singapore 2005

Public Service Award, Government of Singapore 2004

Public Service Star Award, Government of Singapore 2008

Named and Invited Lectures
(not including Conference Keynote Lectures)

1966 Inaugural Lecture as Professor of History at the University of Malaya

1970 Inaugural Flinders Asian Studies Lecture, Flinders University, Adelaide

1974 The Annual Lecture, Australian Academy of the Humanities, Canberra

1979 The 40th George Ernest Morrison Lecture in Ethnology 1979, Canberra

1982 Presidential Lecture, Australian Academy of Humanities, Canberra
      10th Annual Lecture, Korean National Academy of Sciences, Seoul

1989 The Walter E. Edge Lecture, Princeton University

1992 Inaugural International Lecture on the Chinese Overseas, San Francisco

1996 IIAS Annual Lecture, International Institute for Asian Studies (IIAS), Leiden University
      The Annual Lecture, Australian Economics Society, Canberra
      The Ruth Wong Lecture on Education, Singapore

1997 The Edwin O. Reischauer Lectures, Harvard University
      The Wu Teh-yao Lectures on Chinese Culture, Singapore
      The Menzies Oration on Higher Education, The University of Melbourne
      The 11th Panglaykim Memorial Lecture, Jakarta

1998   Sir Edward Dunlop Lecture, AsiaLink, University
       of Melbourne
       The Second Annual East Asia Distinguished Lecture,
       University of Virginia
1999   The Asa Briggs Lecture, The Commonwealth of
       Learning, Brunei
2000   The Smuts Commonwealth Lectures, University of
       Cambridge
2002   The Giri Deshingkar Memorial Lecture, New
       Delhi
2005   The Ishizaka Lectures, Ishizaka Foundation,
       Tokyo
       The Fu Sinian Lectures, Academia Sinica, Taipei
2006   The 10th Annual Gaston Sigur Memorial Lecture,
       George Washington University, Washington DC
       The Inaugural Tsai Lecture, Harvard University
2006   Foundation Lecture, University of Manchester
2008   The Yu Ying-shih Lectures in History, Chinese
       University of Hong Kong
2009   Inaugural Global China Lecture, University of
       California at Los Angeles
       Space for Thought Lecture, London School of
       Economics
2010   University of Denver Bridges to the Future Spring
       Lecture

Current Service and Civic Activities

In Singapore
Institute of Southeast Asian Studies. Chairman of Board
    of Trustees, 2002–

Lee Kuan Yew School of Public Policy, NUS. Chairman of Governing Board, 2005–

East Asian Institute, NUS. Chairman of Management Board, 2007–

MOE Academic Research Fund, Chairman of Expert Panel, 2006–

Member, NUS Asia Research Institute Board, 2000–

Member, Management Committee, NUS Global Asia Institute, 2009–

Member, NUS Institute of South Asian Studies Board, 2005–

Nanyang Technological University (NTU) Chinese Studies Department. Member of International Advisory Board, 2002–

Rajaratnam School of International Studies and Institute of Defence and Strategic Studies, NTU. Member of Board of Governors, 1998–

Chinese Heritage Centre. Vice-Chairman, Board of Governors, 2001–; Member, 1995–2001

Chinese Overseas Databank (HuayiNet). Adviser, 1998–

Network of East Asian Think-tanks (NEAT), Coordinator for Singapore, 2004–

History of Nation-building Project, ISEAS. Coordinator and General Editor 1997–

Senior Fellow, Diplomatic Academy, Ministry of Foreign Affairs

Outside Singapore

Distinguished Fellow, Institute of Humanities and Social Sciences, University of Hong Kong, 2009–

Council Member, The Toyo Bunko 东洋文库 Governing Board, Tokyo, 2007–

White Rose East Asia Centre International Advisory Board, Universities of Leeds and Sheffield, UK. Member, 2007–

Universiti Tunku Abdul Rahman (UTAR), Malaysia. Chairman, International Advisory Board, 2002–

Centre of Asian Studies, The University of Hong Kong. Distinguished Fellow, 1999–

Nalanda Mentor Group, Delhi, Alternate Member, 2007–

Centre for Overseas Chinese Research, Chinese Academy of Social Sciences (Beijing). Advisor, 2002–

Asia-Pacific Research Center, Academia Sinica, Taipei. Advisor, 2003–

World Congress of Library and Institutes for Chinese Overseas Studies. President, 2003–

Asia-Link, University of Melbourne. Co-Patron, 1994–

Canadian Foundation for Innovation, Ottawa. Member, Multidisciplinary Assessment Committee 2000–

International Confucian Association, Beijing. Adviser, 1995–

Jinan University, Guangzhou. Member of Board of Trustees, 1984–

Asia-Pacific Studies Program, Academia Sinica, Taipei. Adviser 2002–

East Asian History of Science Foundation Ltd, Hong Kong. Corresponding Director, 1996–

Studies from the International Institute for Asian Studies Series, Leiden and Amsterdam. Advisor, 1998–

Dictionary of Hong Kong Biography. Member of Editorial Board, 2003–

Member of Editorial Committee, *New Global Studies* 2006–

Corresponding Research Fellow, Institute of Modern History, Academia Sinica, 2008

China: an International Journal. Chairman of Editorial Board, 2007–

Journal of Chinese Overseas. Chairman of Editorial Board, 2006–

The International Journal of Diasporic Chinese Studies. Chairman of Advisory Board, 2008–

Member of Editorial Board or Advisory/Corresponding Editor of the following journals:

—Journal of Southeast Asian Studies (Singapore)
—The China Journal (Canberra)
—The China Quarterly (London) (to 2009)
—Japanese Journal of Political Science (Cambridge)
—Modern Asian Studies (Cambridge)
—Pacific Affairs (Vancouver)
—Journal of the Royal Asiatic Society (London)
—The Pacific Review (Warwick University)
—The Round Table (London)
—Journal of the Malaysian Branch, Royal Asiatic Society (Kuala Lumpur)
—Asian Studies Review (Brisbane)
—China Review (Hong Kong)
—Journal of Comparative Asian Development (Chicago)
—Cambridge Review of International Affairs (Cambridge)
—Asian Culture (Singapore)
—Monde Chinois (Paris)
—China Aktuell, renamed Journal of Current Chinese Affairs (Hamburg)

—Nanda yuyan wenhua xuebao 南大语言文化学报 (Singapore)
—Journal of Malaysian Chinese Studies (Kuala Lumpur)
—Zhongguo shehui keshue jikan 中国社会科学季刊 (Hong Kong)
—The American Asian Review (New York)
—Dongfang wenhua jicheng 东方文化集成 (Eastern Cultures Collection), (Beijing)
—Hong Kong Journal of Modern Chinese History
—East Asia: an International Quarterly (Rutgers University)
—Hong Kong Economic Journal Monthly (Hong Kong)
—Nanfang xueyuan xuebao 南方学院学报 (Skudai, Johor)
—Zhongguo yanjiu 中国研究 (Beijing)

Previous Service and Civic Activities (A Select List)

While in Singapore, 1996–2009

Social Science Research Council, New York. Board Member 1999–2006; Secretary 2001–2006

Asia Scholarship Foundation (formerly Asian Studies in Asia Program, Institute of International Education, New York), Bangkok. Chairman of the Board 1998–2007

United Kingdom Research Assessment 2008. Panel Member, 2006–2009

National University of Singapore (NUS) Council. Member 2000–2004

International Society for the Study of the Chinese Overseas, Berkeley, California. President, 1991–2004

Cambridge University East Asian Institute. Member of Advisory Committee, 1998–2007

Institute of Asian Research, The University of British Columbia. Member of International Advisory Board, 1997–2007

Southeast Asia Research Centre, City University of Hong Kong. Member of Advisory Board, 2001–2007

Tan Kah Kee (Chen Jiageng) International Society. President, 1996–2008

ACCESS Committee, Media Corp. Chairman, 2002–2005

China; an International Journal. Co-editor, 2002–2007

Oxford Maritime History, Oxford University Press. Advisor, 2000–2008

Singapore Documentary History Committee, Member 2003–2006

Education Services Accreditation Council. Chairman 2004–2006

China Studies Syllabus Committee, Ministry of Education. Member 2004–05

NUS Public Policy Programme. Chairman, International Advisory Group 2001–2004

Faculty of Arts and Social Science Review Committee, NUS. Member, 1999–2003

Human Capital Committee, Social Science Research Council, New York. Member 1997–2003

National Library Board, Singapore. Member since 1997–2003

Chairman, Advisory Panel for Chinese Library Services 2000–2003

Institute of Southeast Asian Studies, Singapore. Member of Regional Advisory Council 1982–2002

Chiang Ching-kuo Foundation, Taipei. Member of Review Panel 1991–2002

Southeast Asian Area Studies Program, Academia Sinica, Taipei. Adviser 1994–2002

National Brains Trust on Education, Kuala Lumpur. Member 2002

The International Institute for Strategic Studies (IISS), London. Member of Council 1992–2001

National Arts Council, Singapore. Member 1996–2000

Singapore History Museum. International Adviser, 2004–08

Asia-Pacific Council, Griffith University, Brisbane. Chairman 1997–2000

The National Collection on China and the Chinese Diaspora, Singapore. Chairman of Panel of Advisers 1997–2000

The Encyclopaedia of Singapore. Member of Advisory Board, 2004–2007

National Heritage Board, Singapore. Member 1997–1999; Advisor 1999–2002

The Research Centre for Chinese Studies, NUS. Member of Advisory Panel 1995–1998

Institute of East Asian Philosophies, later Institute of East Asian Political Economy. Member of Board of Directors 1989–97; Chairman 1996–97

While in Hong Kong, 1986–1995

Executive Council, Hong Kong Government. Executive Councillor 1990–92

Environmental Pollution Advisory Committee (EPCOM), Hong Kong. Chairman 1988–93; renamed Advisory Council on the Environment (ACE) in 1993. Chairman 1993–95

Council for the Performing Arts, Hong Kong. Chairman 1989–94

Commission on Remuneration for Members of the Legislative Council, Hong Kong. Chairman 1993–95

International Association of Historians of Asia. President 1988–91

Association of Southeast Asian Institutions of Higher Learning. Administrative Board Member 1986–88. First Vice-President 1990–92

Royal Society of Arts, London. Fellow, Honorary Corresponding Member and Chairman of Hong Kong Chapter 1987–95

Institute of East Asian Philosophies, renamed Institute of East Asian Political Economy in 1991, Singapore. Member of Board of Directors 1989–97

The Chinese University of Hong Kong. Member of Council 1986–95

World Wildlife Fund for Nature, Hong Kong. Executive Council Member 1987–95

East Asian History of Science Foundation Ltd, Hong Kong. Member of Board of Directors 1987–95

Independent Commission Against Corruption (ICAC) Complaints Committee, Hong Kong. Member 1989–95

Asia-Australia Institute, University of New South Wales, Sydney. Member of Council, 1990–94

The Asia Society, Hong Kong Center. Member of Council 1990–95

While in Australia, 1968–1986

Australia-China Council, Canberra. Chairman 1984–86

Australian Academy of the Humanities. President 1980–83

Asian Studies Association of Australia. President 1978–80. Council Member 1976–82

East-West Center, Honolulu. International Advisory Panel Member 1979–91

Committee on Australia-Japan Relations, Canberra. Member 1982–84

While in Malaysia, 1959–1968

Curriculum Review Committee, Nanyang University, Singapore. Chairman 1964–65

International Association of Historians of Asia. President 1964–68

Dewan Bahasa dan Pustaka, Kuala Lumpur. Chairman, Istilah Committee for History, 1967–68

Nanyang Hsueh-hui, Singapore. Councillor and Editor of Journal 1958–67

Royal Asiatic Society, Malayan Branch, Kuala Lumpur. Vice-President and Editor of Journal 1962–68

Commission of Inquiry on Singapore Riots, Malaysia. Member 1964–65

Commission on Traditional Medicine, Kuala Lumpur. Member 1965–68

Professor Wang Gungwu
Select Publications

1950

Pulse. Published by Beda Lim at the University of Malaya, Singapore. 16 pages.

1953

"Chinese Reformists and Revolutionaries in the Straits Settlements, 1900–1911", B.A. Honours Academic Exercise, University of Malaya, Singapore.

"Chinese Historiography: The Standard Histories", *The Historical Journal*, no. 1, University of Malaya History Society, Singapore.

1954

The Nanhai Trade: A Study of the Early History of Chinese Trade in the South China Sea. M.A. thesis, University of Malaya, Singapore.

"Johor Lama: An introduction to archaeology", *The Malayan Historical Journal,* Vol. 1, no. 1, pp. 18–23.

1957

The Structure of Power in North China during the Five Dynasties. Ph.D. Dissertation, University of London School of Oriental and African Studies.

"The *Chiu Wu-Tai Shih* and History-Writing during the Five Dynasties", *Asia Major*, London, pp. 1–22.

1958

The Nanhai Trade: a study of the Early History of Chinese Trade in the South China Sea (Monograph issue of *Journal of Malayan Branch Royal Asiatic Society)*, vol. 31, pt. 2, 135 pages.

"The Chinese in Search of a Base in the Nanyang", *Nanyang Hsueh-pao*, Singapore, pp. 86–98.

"Trial and Error in Malayan poetry", *Malayan Undergrad*, vol. 9, no. 6, July 1958.

"Twelve Poems", in *Litmus One, Selected University Verse, 1949–1957*, The Raffles Society, University of Malaya, Singapore, pp. 27–36.

1959

A Short History of the Nanyang Chinese, Donald Moore, Singapore, 42 pages.

"Sun Yat-sen and Singapore", *Nanyang Hsueh-pao*, Singapore, pp. 55–68.

1960

"An Early Chinese Visitor to Kelantan", *Malaya in History*, vol. 6, no. 1, Kuala Lumpur, pp. 31–35.

"Memperkembang Bahasa Kebangsaan: Peranan Perseorangan dan Badan Kesusasteraan" (Developing the National Language: The role of individuals and literary bodies), *Bahasa*, Kuala Lumpur, pp. 86–95.

1961

"The Emergence of Southeast Asia", *Bakti,* Journal of the Political Study Centre, No. 3, Singapore, pp. 9–11.

"A Letter to Kuala Pilah, 1908", *Malaya in History*, vol. 6, no. 2, Kuala Lumpur, pp. 22–26.

"Mr. Harrison and the 'Western Bias' in the Nanhai Trade", *Asian Perspectives*, Hong Kong

1962

Latar Belakang Kebudayaan Pendudok di-Tanah Melayu: Bahagian Kebudayaan China [The Cultural Background of the Peoples of Malaysia: Chinese Culture], Kuala Lumpur: Dewan Bahasa dan Pustaka. 69 pages.

The New nationalism and the Nanyang Chinese, with special reference to Malaya. Athens: Fourth International Conference on World Politics. 1962. 23 pages.

"Feng Tao, an essay on Confucian loyalty", in *Confucian Personalities*, ed. by Arthur F. Wright and Denis Twitchett. Stanford: Stanford University Press, pp. 123–145, 346–351.

"The Chinese in Southeast Asia", *Commonwealth Journal*, London, vol. 5, no. 2, pp. 85–90.

"Malacca in 1403", *Malaya in History*, vol. 7, no. 2, Kuala Lumpur, pp. 1–5.

"Malayan Nationalism", *Royal Central Asian Journal*, vol. 49, pts. iii and iv, London, pp. 317–325.

"Five Poems", by Awang Kedua, *Varsity 1962*, Kuala Lumpur, pp. 71–72.

1963

The Structure of Power in North China during the Five Dynasties, University of Malaya Press. 257 pages.

"The Melayu in *Hai-kuo Wen-chien Lu*", *Journal of the Historical Society*, University of Malaya, Kuala Lumpur, vol. 2, pp. 1–9.

"The Sino-Turk Alliance in Wu-Tai History", *Journal of the Chinese Language Society*, Kuala Lumpur, pp. 94–106.

1964

Malaysia: a Survey. (Editor) New York and London: Praeger and Pall Mall Press. 466 pages.

"The opening of relations between China and Malacca, 1402–1405", in *Malayan and Indonesian Studies: Festschrift for Richard Winstedt*, edited by J.S. Bastin and R. Roolvink, London: Oxford University Press, pp. 87–104.

"Nation Formation and Regionalism in Southeast Asia", in *South Asia Pacific Crisis: National Development and the World Community,* edited by Margaret Grant. New York: Dodd, Mead & Company, pp. 125–135, 258–272.

"A Short Introduction to Chinese Writing in Malaya", in *Bunga Emas, An Anthology of Contemporary Malaysian Literature*, edited by T. Wignesan. London: Anthony Blond & Kuala Lumpur: Rayirath (Raybooks) Publications. pp. 249–256.

"The Teaching of History in a Southeast Asian Context", in *History Teaching: Its Problems in Malaya*, edited by Zainal Abidin b. A. Wahid, Department of History, University of Malaya, pp. 1–11.

"Feng Tao, an essay on Confucian loyalty", in *Confucianism and Chinese Civilisation*, edited by Arthur F. Wright, New York: Atheneum, 1964, pp. 123–145, 346–351.

(First published in *Confucian Personalities*, ed. by Arthur F. Wright and Denis Twitchett, Stanford: Stanford University Press, pp. 188–210, 344–350)

1965

"The Uniqueness of Europe", in *The Glass Curtain between Europe and Asia*, edited by Raghavan Iyer, London: Oxford University Press, pp. 233–243.

"The Concept of Malaysia", "Early Chinese Influence in Southeast Asia", Political Malaya, 1895–1941", "The Japanese Occupation and Post-war Malaya, 1941–1948", "Malaya: The Road to Independence and Malaysia", in *History of the Malaysian States*, Singapore: Lembaga Gerakan Pelajaran Dewasa, pp. 1–4, 12–16, 80–91.

"Chinese Historians and the Nature of Early Chinese Foreign Relations", *The Journal of the Oriental Society of Australia*, Sydney, pp. 39–54.

"The Vietnam Issue", *Journal of the Historical Society*, University of Malaya, pp. 1–5.

"The Way Ahead", *The Straits Times Annual for 1966*, Singapore, pp. 26–31.

1966

The Use of History, an inaugural lecture at the University of Malaya, December 14, 1966, Kuala Lumpur, 17 pages.

"Malayan Nationalism", in *Malaysia: selected Historical Readings*, edited by John Bastin and Robin W. Winks, Kuala Lumpur: Oxford University Press, pp. 347–351, 352–358.

"Fuhrungsprobleme der Chinesen in Malaya und Singapore", in *Studien zur Entwicklung in Sud- und Ostasien*, edited by B. Grossmann, Frankfurt am Main: Alfred Metzner, pp. 65–80.

"Communism in Asia" Series, *The Asia Magazine*, November to December, 1966: "Asian Communism Now", "The Ingenious Infiltrators", "Have the Reds missed the Boat?", "Vietnam — the Decisive Test", *The Asia Magazine*, Hong Kong, four weekly parts, 13 , 20, 27 November and 11 December.

1967

The Structure of Power in North China during the Five Dynasties, Stanford University Press, 257 pages. (First published by University of Malaya Press, 1963, and reprinted in 1968).

Notes on Malayan education: domesticating the alien. XXVII International Congress of Orientalists, Ann Arbor, Michigan, U.S.A., August 13–19, 1967. 18 pages. Publisher: [S.l.: s.n.], 1967.

"The Growth of a Nation", in *Ten Years of Merdeka*, Kuala Lumpur: Straits Times, August, pp. 3–6.

"The Use of History", in *Journal of the Historical Society*, University of Malaya, vol. 6, 1967/68, pp. 1–12.

"Communism in Asia", *Journal of the Historical Society*, University of Malaya, Kuala Lumpur, pp. 1–12.

"Winstedt in History", in *The Straits Times Annual for 1967*, Singapore, pp. 91–96.

1968

The Cultural Problems of Malaysia in the Context of Southeast Asia (edited, with S.T. Alishabana and X.S. Thaninayagam), Kuala Lumpur: The Malaysian Society of Orientalists. vi + 252 pages.

The Use of History. (Revised edition), Papers in International Studies, Ohio University, Athens, Ohio, 1968.

"Traditional leadership in a New Nation: The Chinese in Malaya and Singapore", in *Leadership and Authority: a symposium*, edited by G. Wijeyewardene, Singapore: University of Malaya Press, pp. 208–222.

"Early Ming relations with Southeast Asia — a background essay", in *The Chinese World Order*, edited by John K. Fairbank, Cambridge, MA.: Harvard University Press, pp. 34–62, 293–299.

"Comment on C. Martin Wilbur, Warlordism in Modern China", in *China in Crisis*, Vol. 1, Book 1, edited by Ho Ping-ti, Chicago: University of Chicago Press, pp. 264–270.

"A New Sensation", in *Twenty-two Malaysian Stories: an anthology of writing in English*, selected and edited by Lloyd Fernando, Heinemann Educational Books (Asia), Singapore, pp. 113–125. [first published in 1952]

"Cultural Tensions in Asia", In *Australia: a Part of Asia?* Papers presented at the symposium at The University of New South Wales on November 7, 1968, Sydney: University of New South Wales, pp. 32–41.

"South and Southeast Asian Historiography", *International Encyclopaedia of the Social Sciences*, Edited by David L. Sills. New York: Macmillan, volume six, pp. 420–428.

"The Uniqueness of Europe", in *Der Glaserne Vorhang Zwischen Asien und Europa*, edited by Raghavan Iyer. Verlag Georg D.W. Callwey, Munich, 1968, pp. 249–260.

"The First Three Rulers of Malacca", *Journal of the Malaysian Branch Royal Asiatic Society*, Singapore, vol. 41, no. 1, pp. 11–22.

1969

Nanyang Hua-jen chien-shih 南洋华人简史 [A Short History of the Nanyang Chinese], translated and annotated by Chong Yit Sun, Taipei: Shui-niu Book Co., 5 + 208 pages.

"Reflections on the Generational Gap in Asia", in *The Generational Gap & Australian-Asian Relations*, edited by J. Jordens, Melbourne: Australian-Asian Association of Victoria, pp. 105–117.

"The University in relation to traditional culture", in *Proceedings of the Asian Workshop on Higher Education*, edited by Li Choh-Ming, Hong Kong: The Chinese University of Hong Kong, pp. 21–32.

"The Compulsion to look South: Asian Awareness of Australia"

(Pacific Signposts no. 5), *Meanjin Quarterly*, Melbourne, vol. 28, no. 116, pp. 49–58.

"Malaysia: An Interim View", *The May Tragedy in Malaysia: A Collection of Essays*, Monash University Malaysia-Singapore Students' Association, pp. 10–13.

1970

Scholarship and the History and Politics of Southeast Asia, Flinders University Asian Studies No. 1, Adelaide, 35 pages.

The Fall of the Manchu Dynasty and the Rise of Chinese Republicanism, University Monographs in History, Sydney University History Club, 22 pages.

"China and Southeast Asia, 1402–1424", in *Social History of China & Southeast Asia*, edited by Jerome Chen and Nicholas Tarling, Cambridge: Cambridge University Press, pp. 375–401.

"'Public' and 'Private' Overseas Trade in Chinese History", in *Societes et Compagnies de Commerce en Orient et dans L'Ocean Indien*, edited by Michel Mollat, Paris: S.E.V.P.E.N. pp. 215–226.

"Chinese politics in Malaya", *The China Quarterly*, London, no. 43, pp. 1–30.

"Malaysia: contending elites", *Current Affairs Bulletin*, Sydney, vol. 47, no. 3, December, pp. 1–12.

"Political Change in Malaysia", *Pacific Community,* Tokyo, vol. 1, no. 4, pp. 687–696.

"Race, religion and nationalism in Asia", *Tenggara*, Kuala Lumpur, no. 5, pp. 93–98.

"The Pier", "Moon thoughts", "Ahmad", "A New Sensation". In *The Flowering Tree: Selected Writings from Singapore/Malaysia*, compiled by Edwin Thumboo, Educational Publications Bureau, Singapore, pp. 21, 22, 23, 123–138.

1971

"Die Kulturen Sudostasiens von 1200 bis 1800", in *Saeculum Weltgeschichte*, Herder, Freiburg, vol. 6, pp. 205–218.

"On the South-Eastern Edge of Asia: an Asian View", in *Everyman in Australia* (Octagon Lectures, 1970), edited by G.C. Bolton, University of Western Australia Press, Perth, pp. 39–53.

"Asia and the Western Experience", *Quadrant*, Sydney, pp. 9–14. (Reprinted in *Quest*, Bombay, 1971)

"Secret Societies and Overseas Chinese" (review article), *The China Quarterly*, London, 47, pp. 553–560.

1972

The Structure of Power in North China during the Five Dynasties. Taipei: Hongqiao shudian (Rainbow-Bridge Book Co.), 257 pages.

Nanyo Kajin shoshi [A Short History of the Nanyang Chinese], Japanese translation. Tokyo: Ajia Keizai Kenkyujo. 54 pages.

"Political Chinese: an aspect of their Contribution to Modern Southeast Asian History", in *Southeast Asia in Modern World*, edited by Bernard Grossman, Wiesbaden: Otto Harrassowitz, pp. 115–128.

"The University and the Commuity" (Keynote & Closing Lectures) in *Proceedings, Second Asian Workshop on Higher Education*, edited by Rayson L. Huang. Singapore: Nanyang University, pp. 17–29, 111–120.

"The Inside and Outside of Chinese History", *The Round Table*, London, pp. 283–295.

1973

Essays on the Sources for Chinese History (editor, with Donald Leslie and Colin Mackerras), Canberra and Columbia, SC.: Australian National University and University of South Carolina Press. xii + 378 pages.

The Re-emergence of China (New Zealand Institute of International Affairs). Wellington, 12 pages.

"The Middle Yangtse in T'ang politics", in *Perspectives on the T'ang*, edited by Arthur F. Wright and Denis Twitchett, New Haven: Yale University Press, pp. 193–255.

"Nationalism in Asia", in *Nationalism: the nature & evolution of an idea*, edited by Eugene Kamenka, Canberra and London: Australian National University Press and Edward Arnold, pp. 82–98.

"Some Comments on the later Standard Histories", in *Essays on the Sources for Chinese History*, edited by Donald D. Leslie, Colin Mackerras & Wang Gungwu, Canberra and Columbia, SC.: Australian National University Press and University South Carolina Press, pp. 53–63.

"Chinese Society and Chinese Foreign Policy", *International Affairs*, London, pp. 616–624. (Reprinted in *Strategic Digest*, Delhi, vol. 3, no. 7, pp. 46–53.)

"Bureacracy in Imperial China", *Public Administration* (Special issue on the Politics of Bureaucracy), Sydney, vol. 32, no. 1, pp. 62–71.

Comments on Soedjatmoko, "The Role of the Medium and Small Nations in the New Asia-Pacific Setting", in *Foreign Policy for Australia: Choices for the Seventies*, Australian Institute of Political Science 39th Summer School, Angus and Robertson, Sydney, pp. 52–58.

1974

The Rebel-Reformer and Modern Chinese Biography, The Annual Lecture to the Australian Academy of the Humanities, Sydney University Press, 23 pages.

(Also published in *Self and Biography: Essays on the Individual and Society in Asia*, 1975; and *Proceedings, 1974, Australian Academy of the Humanities*, Sydney, 1975)

"Chinese Civilisation & the Diffusion of Culture", in *Grafton Elliott-Smith: The Man & His Work*, edited by A.P. Elkin, Sydney: Sydney University Press, pp. 197–209.

"Burning Books and Burying Scholars Alive: Some Recent Interpretations concerning Ch'in Shih-huang", *Papers on Far Eastern History*, Canberra, 9, pp. 137–186.

"Some Aspects of Southeast Asian Attitudes towards Japan", *Bulletin of the International House of Japan*, Tokyo, no. 33, pp. 1–18.

1975

Self and Biography: Essays on the Individual and Society in Asia, Sydney: Sydney University Press. ix + 217 pages.

"The Limits of Nanyang Chinese Nationalism, 1912–1937", in *Southeast Asian History and Historiography:* Essays Presented to D.G.E. Hall, edited by C.D. Cowan and O.W. Wolters, Cornell University Press, London, pp. 405–421.

"The Military Governors and the Decline of the T'ang Dynasty", in *The Making of China: Main Themes in Premodern Chinese History*, edited by Chun-shu Chang. Englewood Cliffs, N.J.: Prentice-Hall, 1975, pp. 211–229.

"Juxtaposing Past and Present in China Today", *The China Quarterly*, London, March, pp. 1–24.

"The Rebel-Reformer and Modern Chinese Biography", in *Self and Biography: Essays on the Individual and Society in Asia*, edited by Wang Gungwu, Sydney University Press, 1975, pp. 185–206.

"The Chinese Minority in Southeast Asia". *Mindanao Journal*, Mindanao State University, Marawi City, vol. II, no. 1, 1975, pp. 5–19.

1976

"'Are Indonesian Chinese Unique?' Some Observations", in *The Chinese in Indonesia*, edited by J. A.C. Mackie, Thomas Nelson, Melbourne, pp. 199–210.

"Chang Fu"; "Fei Hsin"; "Hsia Yuan-chi"; "Huang Fu"; "Ma Huan", in *Dictionary of Ming Biography*, edited by L. Carrington Goodrich and Chao Ying Fang, Vols. I and II, Columbia University Press, New York, pp. 64–67, 440–441, 531–534, 653–656, 1026–1027.

"Nationalism in China before 1949". In *China: The Impact of Revolution, a survey of Twentieth Century China*, edited by Colin Mackerras. Hawthorn: Longman Australia, pp. 46–58.

"The Origins of Civilisation: an Essay on Chinese Scholarship in Transition", *Asian Thought and Society: an International Review*, New York, vol. 1, no. 3, pp. 247–257.

"The Question of the 'Overseas Chinese'", *Southeast Asian Affairs 1976*, Singapore, pp. 101–110.

1977

China and the World since 1949: The Impact of Independence, Modernity and Revolution, London & New York: Macmillan. xi + 190 pages.

(Translated into Spanish, Mexico City, 1979, 244 pages.)

"Mao the Chinese", in *Mao Tse-tung in the Scales of History*, edited by Dick Wilson, Cambridge University Press, Cambridge, (Contemporary China Institute Publications), pp. 272–299.

[Translated and collected in *Waiguo xuezhe ping Mao Zedong* 外国学者评毛泽东 (Foreign Scholars on Mao Zedong). In four volumes. Zhongguo Gongren Publishing, Beijing, 1997, vol. 1: *Zai lishi di tianping shang* 在历史的天平上 (On the Scales of History), pp. 138–165.]

"A note on the Origins of Hua-ch'iao", *Masalah-Masalah International Masakini*, edited by Lie Tek Tjeng, vol. 7, Jakarta, Lembaga Research Kebudayaan Nasional L.I.P.I., pp. 71–78.

"Empires Unposses'd", *Hemisphere*, Canberra, Vol. 21, No. 4, April, pp. 2–12.

1978

The Chinese Minority in Southeast Asia. Singapore, Chopmen Enterprise. Southeast Asia Research Paper Series 1, Southeast Asian Studies Programme, Nanyang University, Singapore. 16 pages.

(Also published in *Mindanao Journal*, Mindanao State University, Marawi City, vol. II, no. 1, 1975, pp. 5–19.)

Latar Belakang Kebudayaan Pendudok di-Tanah Melayu: Bahagian Kebudayaan China [The Cultural Background of the Peoples of Malaysia: Chinese Culture], Republished, Kuala Lumpur: Dewan Bahasa dan Pustaka, 1978. 69 pages.

"Recent Reinterpretations of History", in *Zhongguo zhuantan wenji* 中国专谈文集, edited by Lu Hanyao 盧漢耀, Hong Kong University Students' Union, Hong Kong, pp. 11–38.

(Also published in *China: Development and Challenge.* Proceedings of the Fifth Leverhulme Conference, edited by Lee Ngok and Lueng Chi-keung. vol. I, 1979.)

Biographies of Han Tung, Li Ch'ung-chin, Li Yun and P'an Mei, in *Sung Biographies*, edited by Herbert Franke, Franz Steiner Verlag, Wiesbaden, (4 volumes), pp. 384–387; pp. 546–549, 597 and 818–821.

"China-Vietnam: Nostalgia for, Rejection of, the Past", in *The Vietnam-Kampuchea-China Conflicts: Motivations, Background, Significance*, edited by M. Salmon, Department of Political and Social Change, Research School of Pacific Studies, Australian National University, Canberra, pp. 42–51.

"Jiu Wudai shi ji Wudai shiqi di lishi zhuanxie 旧五代史及五代时期的历史撰写", *Shih-huo yueh-k'an* 食货月刊, Taipei, vol. 8, no. 5, pp. 237–247.

(Chinese translation of "The Chiu Wu-Tai Shih and History-Writing during the Five Dynasties", *Asia Major*, London.)

1979

China y el Mundo desde 1949: Los efectos de la Independencia, la Modernidad y la Revolucion (Spanish translation of *China and the World since 1949*), Mexico 11, DF. Editorial El Manual Moderno, 244 pages.

"The Chinese Overseas", in *Mouvements de Populations dans L'Ocean Indien*, Actes du Quatrieme Congres de l'Association Historique Internationale de l'Ocean Indien, (1972), Paris: Libraire Honore Champion, pp. 451–457.

"Recent Reinterpretations of History", in *China: Development and Challenge* (Proceedings of the Fifth Leverhulme Conference, Hong Kong, December 1977), edited by Lee Ngok and Lueng Chi-keung. vol. I, edited by W.S.K. Waung, Hong Kong, pp. 3–18.

"The Writing of Pre-modern history in Modern China", in *Proceedings: Seventh Conference of Asian Historians, Bangkok*, vol. 2, pp. 1405–1429.

"Change and More Change in Asia: Thoughts on Recent History", in *Public Lectures, 1977–1978*, International Asian Studies Programme, Chinese University of Hong Kong with Yale-China Association, pp. 14–23.

"Between One and Many: Pluralism in Post-Colonial Societies", in *Cultural Pluralism and the Humanities,* Proceedings, 1979 Humanities Conference, Honolulu: Hawaii Committee for the Humanities, pp. 4–7.

"China and the Region in Relation to Chinese Minorities", *Contemporary Southeast Asia*, Singapore, vol. 1, no. 1, pp. 36–50.

"May Fourth and the GPCR: The Cultural Revolution Remedy", *Pacific Affairs*, Vancouver, 52 (4), pp. 674–690.

1980

Power, Rights and Duties in Chinese History. The 40th George Ernest Morrison Lecture in Ethnology 1979. The Australian National University, Canberra, 30 pages.

[Also published in *Australian Journal of Chinese Affairs*, no. 3, pp. 1–26.]

Hong Kong: Dilemmas of Growth (Editor, with C.K. Leung and Jennifer W. Cushman), Research School of Pacific Studies, Australian National University, Canberra and Centre of Asian Studies, University of Hong Kong, ix + 655 pages.

"The Chinese and the Countries across the Indian Ocean", *Historical relations across the Indian Ocean: Report and papers of the meeting of experts organized by Unesco at Port Louis, Mauritius, from 15 to 19 July 1974.* Paris: UNESCO, 1980, pp. 61–67.

"Some Reflections on Hong Kong's Regional Role and Cultural Identity", in *Hong Kong: Dilemmas of Growth*, edited by C.K. Leung, J.W. Cushman and Wang Gungwu, Research School of Pacific Studies, Australian National University and Centre of Asian Studies, University of Hong Kong, pp. 649–653.

"The Study of the Southeast Asian Past", in *Perceptions of the Past in Southeast Asia*, edited by A.J.S. Reid and David Marr, Singapore: Heinemann, for Asian Studies Association of Australia, pp. 1–8.

1981

Community and Nation: Essays on Southeast Asia and the Chinese, Kuala Lumpur and Sydney: Heinemann Asia and Allen and Unwin. ix + 292 pages.

Society and the Writer: Essays on Literature in Modern Asia (Editor, with M. Guerrero & David Marr), Canberra: Research School of Pacific Studies, Australian National University. v + 322 pages.

"Introduction", in *Southeast Asian Studies in China: A Report*, by Wang Gungwu, J.A.C. Mackie, A.J.S. Reid, D. Marr, I.F.H. Wilson, P. McCawley, J.J. Fox & G. Jones, Canberra: Research School of Pacific Studies, Australian National University, pp. 1–9.

"Southeast Asian Hua-ch'iao in Chinese History-Writing", *Journal of Southeast Asian Studies*, Singapore, vol. 12, no. 1, pp. 1–14.

"Guanyu huaqiaoshi di yixie wenti 关于华侨史的一些问题" (On some questions of Overseas Chinese history), *Nanyang Wenti — liushi zhounian xiaoqing ji jiansuo ershiwuzhounian jinian tekan, diyiji 南洋问题 — 六十周年校庆及建所二十五周年纪念特刊, 第一集* (Southeast Asian Problems, Commemorative volume for the University's 60th anniversary and the Institute's 25th anniversary, vol. 1), Xiamen University Nanyang Research Institute, pp. 92–104.

1982

"The Rhetoric of a Lesser Empire: Early Sung Relations with its Neighbours", in *China Among Equals: The Middle Kingdom and its Neighbours, 10th–14th Centuries*, edited by Morris Rossabi. Berkeley, University of California Press, pp. 47–65.

"Introduction: The Chineseness of China"; "External China", "Five Dynasties and Ten Kingdoms, 907–959; Tangut empire [Xi Xia dynasty]; Khitan empire [Liao dynasty]", in *The Cambridge Encyclopaedia of China*, edited by Brian Hook, Cambridge: Cambridge University Press, pp. 31–34; 104–110; 193–196.

"The interests of Revolutionary China: An overview", in *International Security in the Southeast Asian and Southwest Pacific Region*, edited by Tom B. Miller. St. Lucia: University of Queensland Press, pp. 78–91.

(Also published in *Dong-a Yonkyu* [East Asian Research], Seoul, 1983, pp. 71–87.)

"Interdependence and Moral Order: China's Historical Experience", in *Essays in Commemoration of the Golden Jubilee of the Fung Ping Shan Library (1923–1982)*, edited by Chan Ping-leung et al., Hong Kong: Hong Kong University Press, pp. 406–414.

"Human Values, Science and Learning from History", in *Proceedings: The Xth International Symposia*, Seoul: Korea National Academy of Sciences, pp. 79–98.

"Introduction: ASEAN between Tradition and Modernity", in *Understanding ASEAN*, edited by Alison Broinowski. London: Macmillan, 1982, pp. 1–7.

1983

The Chinese Intellectual — Past & Present. Faculty of Arts Public Lecture. Singapore: National University of Singapore. 30 pages.

"Strong China, Weak China: What Has Changed?" in *When Patterns Change: Turning Points in International Politics*, edited by Nissan Oren. New York and Jerusalem: St. Martin's Press and Magnes Press of Hebrew University, pp. 193–207.

"China and Southeast Asia: some Recent Developments", in *Collected Essays in Sinology, dedicated to Professor Kim Jun-yop*, Seoul: Korea University Press. pp. 657–671.

1984

"Southeast Asia between the 13th and 18th Centuries: Some Reflections on Political Fragmentation and Cultural Change", in *Historia: Essays in Commemoration*, edited by A.B. Muhammad, A. Kaur and Abdullah Zakaria, Kuala Lumpur: Malaysian Historical Society, pp. 1–12.

"The Chinese Urge to Civilize: Reflections on Change", *Journal of Asian History* (Wiesbaden), vol. 18, no. 1, pp. 1–34.

"'State of the art' Surveys of Asian Studies: History, part II" (with Harold Bolitho, Nicholas Tarling, Tony Day, Tom Fisher). *Asian Studies Review*, Volume 8, Issue 2 November 1984, pp. 1–14

1985

The China-Japan Relationship: Implications for Australia. Sydney: Centre of Asian Studies, University of Sydney, 12 pages.

"Loving the Ancient in China", in *Who Owns the Past?* edited by Isabel McBryde, Melbourne: Oxford University Press, pp. 175–195.

"External China as a new Policy Area", *Pacific Affairs*, Vancouver, vol. 58, no. 1 (Spring), pp. 28–43.

"South China Perspectives on Overseas Chinese", *Australian Journal of Chinese Affairs*, Canberra, no. 13, January, pp. 69–84.

"Migration Patterns in History: Malaysia and the Region", *Journal of the Malaysian Branch of the Royal Asiatic Society*, Kuala Lumpur, LVIII/I (no. 248), pp. 43–57.

"Two New Sources of Hokkien Local History", *Asian Studies Association of Australia Review*, Sydney, vol. 8, no. 3, pp. 54–59.

"Asia in Australian Education", in *Addresses at the Amalgamation Conference of the Heads of the Independent Schools of Australia*, Canberra, August 25–30, pp. 37–45.

[Stephen FitzGerald, "Wang Gungwu in Australia", *Australian Studies Association Review*, vol. 10, no. 1, July, pp. 43–48.]

1986

"Reflections on Malaysian Elites" *Review of Indonesian and Malay Studies*, Sydney, vol. 20, no. 1, pp. 100–128.

"Introduction", in *Southeast Asia in the Ninth to Fourteenth Centuries*, edited by David G. Marr and Anthony C. Milner. Singapore and Canberra: Institute of Southeast Asian Studies and Research School of Pacific Studies, Australian National University, pp. xi–xviii.

"Cultural Interpreters", in *Australian Diplomacy: challenges and options*, edited by Anthony C. Milner and Trevor Wilson, Canberra: Australian Institute of International Affairs, pp. 73–76.

1987

Dongnanya Yu Huaren: Wang Gungwu jiaoshou lunwen xuanji 东南亚与华人: 王赓武教授论文选集 [Southeast Asia and the Chinese], translated by Yao Nan. Beijing: Youyi Publisher. 6 + 267 pages.

Language atlas of China. (with Stephen A. Wurm, Liu Yongquan, Benjamin T'sou, Li Rong). Hong Kong: Longman Group.

"Pre-modern history: some trends in writing the history of the Song dynasty (Tenth-Thirteenth Centuries)", in *New Directions in the Social Sciences and Humanities in China*, edited by Michael B. Yahuda, London: Macmillan, pp. 1–27.

"Ethnicity and Religion in Social Development", in *The ASEAN Success Story: social, economic & political dimensions*, edited by Linda G. Martin. Honolulu: East-West Center, pp. 40–43.

"The Scholar in Chinese Society: Historical background", *Asian Culture*, Singapore, vol. 9, pp. 141–151.

1988

Nanhai Maoyi Yu Nanyang Huaren 南海贸易与南洋华人 [The Nanhai Trade and Southeast Asian Chinese], translated by Yao Nan. Hong Kong: Chung-hua Book, Co. 8 + 295 pages

(Chinese translation of *The Nanhai Trade: a study of the Early History of Chinese Trade in the South China Sea*; and *A Short History of the Nanyang Chinese*)

Changing Identities of Southeast Asian Chinese since World War II (with J. Cushman), Hong Kong: Hong Kong University Press. xi + 344 pages.

Trade and Cultural Values: Australia and the Four Dragons, Melbourne: Asian Studies Association of Australia (Current Issues no. 1). 16 pages.

(Also published in *Asian Studies Association of Australia Review*, Sydney, vol. 11, no. 3, pp. 1–10.)

"The Study of Chinese Identities in Southeast Asia", in *Changing Identities of the Southeast Asian Chinese since World War II*, edited by Jennifer Cushman and Wang Gungwu, Hong Kong: Hong Kong University Press, pp. 1–21.

"The Life of William Liu: Australian and Chinese Perspectives", in *Stories of Australian Migration*, edited by John Hardy. Sydney: New South Wales University Press, with the Australian Academy of the Humanities, pp. 109–124.

1989

The Culture of Chinese Merchants, Toronto: Toronto & York University Joint Centre for Asia Pacific Studies (Working Paper Series No. 57). 22 pages.

"Sung-Yuan-Ming relations with Southeast Asia: some comparisons", in *Proceedings: 2nd International Conference on Sinology: Section on History and Archaeology* (December 29–31, 1986), vol. 2, Taipei: Academia Sinica, pp. 1115–1128.

"Tonghua, guihua, and overseas Chinese history (in Chinese)", in *Liangci shijie dazhan qijian zai yazhou zhi haiwai huaren* 两次世界大战期间在亚洲之海外华人 (Overseas Chinese in Asia between the Two World Wars), edited by N.H. Ng Lun and C.Y. Chang 吴伦霓霞、郑赤琰. Hong Kong: Centre for Contemporary Asian Studies, The Chinese University of Hong Kong, pp. 11–23.

"Zhongguo geming zhi wai 中国革命之外" (Outside the Chinese Revolution). In *Zhongguo hequ hecong: haiwai xuezhe de fansi* 中国何去何从: 海外学者的反思 (The Future of China — The Scholars' Views). Teaneck, N.J.: Global Publishing, pp. 1–19.

"Lu Xun, Lim Boon Keng and Confucianism", *Papers on Far Eastern History*, Canberra, no. 39, pp. 75–91.

"The Use of History", in *Syarahan Perdana: dua lima tahun pertama, Fakultas Sastra dan Sains Sosial, 1959–84*, edited by Ungku A. Aziz and Sharil Talib, Jabatan Penerbitan Universiti Malaya, Kuala Lumpur, pp. 255–271.

(First published as an inaugural lecture at the University of Malaya, December 14, 1966, Kuala Lumpur.)

1990

Lishi di Gongneng 历史的功能 [The Function of History], translated by Yao Nan 姚楠. Hong Kong: Chung-hua Book Co. 3 + 240 pages.

"Patterns of Chinese migration in historical perspective", in *Observing Change in Asia — Essays in Honour of J.A.C. Mackie*, edited by R.J. May and W.J. O'Malley, Bathurst: Crawford House Press, pp. 33–48.

"Merchants Without Empire: the Hokkien sojourning communities", in *The Rise of Merchant Empires: Long-Distance Trade in the Early Modern World, 1350–1750*, edited by James D. Tracy, Cambridge: Cambridge University Press, pp. 400–421.

"The Chinese as Immigrants and Settlers", in *Management of Success: the Moulding of Modern Singapore*, edited by K.S. Sandhu and Paul Wheatley, Singapore: Institute of Southeast Asian Studies, pp. 552–562.

"Children in Chinese migration history", in *Children and Migration: A New Challenge for World-wide Social Services*, Proceedings of an International Symposium, Hong Kong, pp. 15–24.

"Outside the Chinese Revolution", *Australian Journal of Chinese Affairs*, Canberra, no. 23, pp. 33–48.

"五百年前的中国与世界 Wubai nianqian di Zhongguo yu shijie" (China and the World 500 years ago), *Ershiyi shiji* 二十一世纪 (Twenty-first century), Hong Kong, no. 2, 1990, pp. 91–100.

"Daode yu falu 道德与法律" (Morality and Law, 1990); "Weishan zhi nan 为善之难" (The difficulty to do good, 1987), in *Huisi: deyu linian yu shijian* 汇思: 德育理念与实践 (Moral Ideas and Practice). Longman, Hong Kong, pp. 7–11, 12–16.

1991

China and the Chinese Overseas. Singapore: Times Academic Press. 7 + 312 pages.

The Chineseness of China: Selected Essays, Hong Kong: Oxford University Press. 12 + 354 pages.

"Ming Foreign Relations: Southeast Asia", in Wang Gungwu, *China and the Chinese Overseas,* pp. 41–78.

"Little Dragons on the Confucian Periphery", in Wang Gungwu, *China and the Chinese Overseas,* pp. 258–272.

"Education in External China", in Wang Gungwu, *China and the Chinese Overseas,* pp. 273–284.

"Among Non-Chinese", *Daedalus, Journal of the American Academy of Arts and Sciences,* Cambridge, Mass., Spring, pp. 135–157.

[Republished as *The Living Tree: The Changing Meaning of Being Chinese Today,* edited by Tu Wei-ming, Stanford University Press, 1994, pp. 127–146.]

"China: 1989 in Perspective", *Southeast Asian Affairs 1990,* Singapore, pp. 71–85.

1992

Community and Nation: China, Southeast Asia and Australia, St Leonard's, NSW: Allen & Unwin Pty Ltd. viii + 359 pages. (New edition of *Community and Nation: Essays on Southeast Asia and the Chinese,* 1981.)

"Universities in Transition in Asia", *Oxford Review of Education,* Oxford, Vol. 18, no. 1, pp. 17–2.

Comments on "The Traditions of the University" by Walter Ruegg, *Minerva: a review of science, learning and policy,* London, vol. 30, no. 2, pp. 234–237, 286–287.

"The Australia Asians Might Not See", *Australian Quarterly,* vol. 64, no. 4, Summer 1992, pp. 350–358.

"Australia's Identity in Asia", in *The Sydney Papers,* vol. 4, no. 4, pp. 45–53, 124–127.

1993

"Migration and Its Enemies", in *Conceptualizing Global History,* edited by Bruce Mazlish and Ralph Buultjens, Boulder, CO.: Westview Press, pp. 131–151.

(A revised version was included in *Culture, Dvelopment, and Democracy: The role of the intellectual*, 1994.)

"China's Overseas World during the Reign of Yongle (1402–1424)", in *A Festchrift in Honour of Professor Jao Tsung-i on the Occasion of His 75th Anniversary*, Hong Kong: Institute of Chinese Studies, The Chinese University of Hong Kong, pp. 281–292.

"Wealth and Culture: Strategies for a Chinese Entrepreneur", in *A Special Brew: essays in honour of Kristof Glamann*, edited by Thomas Riis. Odense: Odense University Press, pp. 405–422.

"To Reform a Revolution: Under the Righteous Mandate", in *Daedalus, Journal of the American Academy of Arts and Sciences*, Cambridge, Mass., Spring, pp. 71–94.

(Republished as *China in Transformation*, edited by Tu Wei-ming, Harvard University Press, pp. 71–94.)

"Greater China and the Chinese Overseas", *The China Quarterly*, London, 136: 926–948.

(Republished as *Greater China*, edited by David Shambaugh, Oxford University Press, London, pp. 274–296.)

"The Status of Overseas Chinese Studies", *Chinese America: History and Perspectives 1994*, Chinese Historical Society of America, San Francisco, pp. 1–18.

The Chinese Diaspora and the Development of China. Hong Kong: Asia Society Hong Kong Centre, 1993, 13 pages.

"C.P. FitzGerald 1902–1992 — In Memoriam", *Australian Journal of Chinese Affairs*, No. 26, pp. 161–163.

"Haiwai huaren yanjiu di diwei 海外华人研究的地位" (The Status of Overseas Chinese Studies), *Huaqiao huaren lishi yanjiu* 华侨华人历史研究 (Historical Research on the Overseas Chinese), Beijing, No. 22, pp. 1–8.

"Meiyou diguo di shangren: qiaoju haiwai di Minnan ren 没有帝国的商人 — 侨居海外的闽南人", *Haijiaoshi yanjiu* 海交史研究 (Research into China Overseas Communications History), Quanzhou, 1993, no. 23, pp. 111–125.

(Translation of "Merchants Without Empire: the Hokkien sojourning communities", 1990.)

1994

Zhongguo yu Haiwai Huaren 中国与海外华人, translated by Tianjin Bianyi Zhongxin 天津编译中心, Hong Kong: Shangwu (Commercial) Press. xi + 366 pages. (Translation of *China and the Chinese Overseas*, Singapore, 1991.)

"Empires and Anti-empires: Asia in World Politics", in *The Fall of Great Powers — Peace, Stability, and Legitimacy*, edited by Geir Lundestad (Nobel Symposium no. 87), Oslo and New York: Scandinavian University Press and Oxford University Press, pp. 235–258.

"The Australia Asians Might Not See", and "Australia's Identity in Asia", in *Australia in the World: Perceptions and Possibilities*, edited by Don Grant and Graham Seal, Perth: Black Swan Press and Curtin University of Technology, pp. 233–238 and pp. 239–243.

(Also published in *Australian Quarterly*, vol. 64, no. 4, Summer 1992, pp. 350–358; and *The Sydney Papers*, vol. 4, no. 4, pp. 45–53, 124–127.)

"The University as a Global Institution", in *The Universities of the Future: Roles in the Changing World Order* (The First Richard, A. Harvill Conference on Higher Education, University of Arizona, November, 1992), Tucson, Arizona, pp. 38–43.

The Modern Chinese Experience of Reform. Hobart: Universtiy of Tasmania Asia Centre, 1994.

"Global Development and the Movement of Peoples", in *Culture, Development, and Democracy: The role of the intellectual*, edited by Selo Soemardjan and Kenneth W. Thompson, Tokyo: United Nations University Press, Tokyo, pp. 207–223.

"Guanyu Wenhua Zhongguo di Sige Yiwen 关于文化中国的四个疑问 (Four Questions about Cultural China)", in *Wenhua Zhongguo: Linian yu Shijian* 文化中国: 理念与实践 (Cultural China: the concept and the reality), edited by Chen Chi-nan and Chou Ying-hsiung, Taipei: Asian Culture Co., pp. 3–10.

"Southeast Asian Chinese and the Development of China", *Asian Journal of Political Science*, Singapore, vol. 2, no. 2, pp. 1–19.

(Also published in *Southeast Asian Chinese and China: The Politico-Economic Dimension*, edited by Leo Suryadinata, Times Academic Press, Singapore, pp. 12–30.)

"The Hakka in Migration History", in *Kejia Yanjiu Jikan* 客家研究 季刊 (Journal of Hakka Studies), no. 5, pp. 1–39.

(Also in *The Proceedings of the International Conference on Hakkaology*, edited by Hsieh Chien and C.Y. Chang, 1995.)

"Commemorative Lecture", in *The Commemorative Lectures*, Fukuoka Asian Cultural Prizes 1994, Fukuoka City, pp. 35–46.

1995

The Chinese Way: China's Position in International Relations (Nobel Institute Lectures 1995). Oslo: Scandinavian University Press. 89 pages.

Hong Kong's Transition: A Decade after the Deal (editor, with Wong Siu-lun). Hong Kong: Oxford University Press. xv + 163 pages.

"Southeast Asian Chinese and the Development of China", in *Southeast Asian Chinese and China: The Politico-Economic Dimension*, edited by Leo Suryadinata, Times Academic Press, Singapore, pp. 12–30.

"East-West Cultural Encounters: Reflections on Conflicts and Convergences", *K-FACE*, Kanagawa, vol. 1, no. 1, pp. 63–73.

1996

The Revival of Chinese Nationalism (IISS Lecture). Leiden: International Institute for Asian Studies. 26 pages.

National Choice, Pacific Economic Papers No. 260. Canberra: Australia-Japan Research Centre. 6 pages. Also published in, *Asian Studies Review* (Melbourne), vol. 20, No. 2, pp. 1–6.

"Sojourning: The Chinese Experience in Southeast Asia", in *Sojourners and Settlers: Histories of Southeast Asia and the Chinese*, edited by Anthony Reid, St Leonard's, NSW: Allen & Unwin, pp. 1–14. [Republished in Honolulu by University of Hawaii Press in 2001.]

"Openness and Nationalism: Outside the Chinese Revolution", in

Chinese Nationalism, edited by Jonathan Unger, Armonk, NY: M.E. Sharpe, pp. 113–125.

"Merchants Without Empire: the Hokkien sojourning communities", in *Merchant networks in the early modern world, 1450–1800*, edited by Sanjay Subrahmanyam, Aldershot, GB and Brookfield, Vt.: Variorum, pp. 50–71.

(First published in *The Rise of Merchants Empires: Long-Distance Trade in the Early Modern World, 1350–1750*, edited by James D. Tracy, pp. 400–421.)

"A Machiavelli for Our Times" (Review Article on Samuel Huntington's *The Clash of Civilzations*), *The National Interest* (Washington), no. 46, Winter, pp. 69–73.

"Upgrading the Migrant: Neither *Huaqiao* Nor *Huaren*", in *Chinese America: History and Perspectives 1996*, Chinese Historical Society of America, San Francisco, 1996, pp. 1–18. (Also in *China em Estudo* (Zhonghua xuezhi), Sao Paulo, pp. 9–23.)

1997

Global History and Migrations (Editor), Boulder, CO.: Westview Press. 309 pages.

Xianggang shi xinbian 香港史新编 [Hong Kong History: New Perspectives]. (Editor) Two volumes. Hong Kong: Joint Publications. 903 pages. (Volume One: 416 pages; Volume Two: 487 pages.)

Hong Kong in the Asia-Pacific Region: Rising to the New Challenges (Editor, with Wong Siu-lun). Hong Kong: Centre of Asian Studies, University of Hong Kong. 166 pages.

Dynamic Hong Kong: Business and Culture (Editor, with Wong Siu-lun). Hong Kong: Centre of Asian Studies, University of Hong Kong. 272 pages.

Nationalism and Confucianism, and *Haiwai Huaren di Minzu zhuyi* 海外华人的民族主义 (The Nationalism of the Chinese Overseas). The Wu Teh-yao Lectures, Singapore: UniPress, Centre for the Arts, National University of Singapore. 64 pages.

The Modern University in Australia and Asia, The Menzies Oration on Higher Education, 1 October 1996, University of Melbourne. 22 pages.

China's Place in the Region: The Search for Allies and Friends, The 1997 Panglaykim Memorial Lecture, Center for Strategic and International Studies, Jakarta. 20 pages. (Also published in *The Indonesia Quarterly*, Vol. 25, No. 4.)

"Migration History: Some Patterns Revisited", in *Global History and Migrations*, edited by Wang Gungwu, Boulder, CO.: Westview Press, pp. 1–22.

"Chinese Civilisation in Historical Perspective", *The Chinese Collections*, Singapore: Asian Civilisations Museum, National Heritage Board, pp. 13–23.

"Xianggang xiandai shehui 香港现代社会 (Modern Hong Kong Society)", in *Xianggang shi xinbian* 香港史新编 [Hong Kong History: New Perspectives], edited by Wang Gungwu, Two volumes, Joint Publications, Hong Kong. Vol. I, "Preface", pp. 1–2; and vol. 2, pp. 859–867.

"Hong Kong as the Home of China Coast Chinese: An Historical Perspective", in *Hong Kong in the Asia-Pacific Region*, edited by Wang Gungwu and Wong Siu-lun, Centre of Asian Studies, Hong Kong, pp. 145-166.

"Hua-shang wen-hua te yen-chiu 华商文化的研究" (The Study of Chinese Merchant Culture), in *Chung-kuo hai-yang fa-chan shih lun-wen chi* 中国海洋发展史论文集, sixth collection, edited by Chang Yen-hsien. Nan-kang: Chung-yang yen-chiu yuan Chung-shan jen-wen she-hui k'e-hsueh yen-chiu so, pp. 1–7.

"The Significance of Confucianism in Chinese Culture: Past and Present", in Osman Bakar and Cheng Gek Nai (eds.), *Islam and Confucianism: A Civilizational Dialogue*. Kuala Lumpur: Centre for Civilizational Dialogue, University of Malaya, pp. 191–204.

"Haiwai Huaren yu Minzu Zhuyi 海外华人与民族主义" (The Nationalism of the Chinese Overseas), in *Sun Wen yu Huaqiao (Sun Yat-sen and the Overseas Chinese: Jinian Sun Zhongshan*

danchen 130 zhounian guoji xuexhu taolunhui lunwenji 孙文与
华侨: 纪念孙中山诞辰*130*周年国际学术讨论会论文集. Kobe:
Sun Zhongshan jinianhui, pp. 5–19.

"Ajia ni okeru daigaku to toshi no patonashipu" (City and Region:
The Role of Universities in Asia), in *Kokusaika suru toshi to
daigaku,* Proceedings of Conference on Universities and Cities,
Fukuoka, pp. 21–23, 78–87.

"National Education and the Scientific Tradition", The Ruth Wong
Lecture, 26 November 1996, Singapore. In *The Australian
Educational Researcher*, vol. 24, no. 1, pp. 49–62.

(Also in Jill Blackmore and Toh Kok Aun (eds.), *Educational
Research: Building New Partnerships*. Singapore: Educational
Research Association, pp. 49–62.)

"Tan Xianggang zhengzhi bianqian 谈香港政治变迁 (Coping with
Political Change), *Ershiyi shiji,* Hong Kong, no. 41, June,
pp. 76–82.

1998

*The Nanhai Trade: The Early History of Chinese Trade in the South
China Sea.* New edition. Singapore: Times Academic Press.
134 pages.)

(First published in *Journal of the Malayan Branch of the Royal
Asiatic Society*, 1958)

The Chinese Diaspora: Selected Essays (Edited, with Wang Ling-chi).
Two volumes. Singapore: Times Academic Press. Volume One:
290 pages; Volume Two: 300 pages.

China's Political Economy (Editor, with John Wong). Singapore:
Singapore University Press and World Scientific. 373 pages.

Minzu zhuyi zai Zhongguo di fuxing 民族主义在中国的复兴. Singapore
Dongya Lunwen (East Asian Institute Working Papers), No. 1.
20 pages.

(Translation of *The Revival of Chinese Nationalism*).

"Introduction: Migration and New National Identities"; and
    "Upgrading the Migrant: Neither Huaqiao nor Huaren". In *The
    Last Half Century of Chinese Overseas*, edited by Elizabeth

Sinn. Hong Kong: Hong Kong University Press, pp. 1–12; 15–33.

"Ming Foreign Relations: Southeast Asia". In *The Cambridge History of China, vol. 8: The Ming Dynasty, 1368–1644, Part 2*, edited by Denis Twitchett and Frederick W. Mote. Cambridge and New York: Cambridge University Press, pp. 301–332, and 992–995.

"Introduction"; and "Nationalism among the overseas Chinese". In *The Encyclopedia of the Chinese Overseas*. Edited by Lynn Pan. Cambridge, MA: Harvard University Press; and Singapore: Archipelago Press and Landmark Books. [Chinese edition, "Daolun 导论"; and "Haiwai huaren di minzu zhuyi 海外华人的民族主义", in *Haiwai Huaren Baike Quanshu 海外华人百科全书*. Hong Kong: Joint Publishing Co.], pp. 10–13; 102–105.]

"Commentary on Wolf Lepenies' *The End of the Cultural Westernisation of the World*? Singapore: Goethe Institut and Asia-Europe Foundation, pp. 21–31.

"Singapore at the Crossroads of Civilization". In *Singapore: Re-Engineering Success*. Edited by Arun Mahizhnan and Lee Tsao Yuan. Singapore: The Institute of Policy Studies and Oxford University Press, pp. 10–18.

"The Status of Overseas Chinese Studies". In *The Chinese Diaspora: Selected Essays*. Edited by Wang Ling-chi and Wang Gungwu. Two volumes. Singapore: Times Academic Press, pp. 1–12.

"Allies et amis: le poids de la culture dans les relations en Asie Pacifique"; and "La place de la Chine dans la region Asie-Pacifique". In *Les relations internationales en Asie-Pacifique*, edited by Xavier Walter. Paris: Alban Editions. Translation by Xavier Walter, pp. 17–36; 63–79.

"China's New Paths for National Re-emergence". In *China's Political Economy*, edited by Wang Gungwu and John Wong, pp. 95–147.

"Xin Jiu minzuzhuyi yu haiwai huaren 新旧民族主义与海外华人". In *Shiji zhi jiao di haiwai huaren 世纪之交的海外华人*, edited by Zhuang Guotu 庄国土 et al. Fuzhou: Renmin Publishing. In two volumes. Vol. One, pp. 1–9.

"Tan Xianggang zhengzhi bianqian 谈香港政治变迁" (Coping with Political Change in Hong Kong).. In *Zhuanhua zhong di Xianggang: shenfen yu zhixu di zaixunqiu* 转化中的香港: 身份与秩序的再寻求, edited by Liu Qingfeng and Guan Xiaochun. Hong Kong: CUHK Press, pp. 31–42.

"Allies and Friends: Culture in Asia-Pacific State Relations", *Asian Journal of Political Science*, vol. 5, no. 2, pp. 23–36.

"Malaysia-Singapore: Two Kinds of Ethnic Transformations", *Southeast Asian Journal of Social Science*, vol. 25, no. 2, pp. 183–187.

"Nationalism, Ethnicity and the Asia Pacific", *Public Policy* (Manila), vol. II, no. 2, April–June, pp. 13–36.

1999

China and Southeast Asia: Myths, Threats, and Culture. (East Asia Institute Occasional Papers, no. 13). Singapore: World Scientific and Singapore University Press. 79 pages.

Hong Kong in China: The Challenges of Transition (Editor, with John Wong). Singapore: Times Academic Press. 324 pages.

China: Two Decades of Reform and Change (Editor, with John Wong). Singapore: Singapore University Press and World Scientific. 172 pages.

Asia: Official Documents 1945–65 on CD-ROM: selected documents from the end of World War II to Vietnam (Editor, with Michael Kandiah, Gillian Starck, Anthony Best, John Saltford, et al.). London: Routledge with Public Records Office, 1999. Six discs.

Towards a New Millennium: Building on Hong Kong's Strengths. (Editor, with Wong Siu-lun). Hong Kong: Centre of Asian Studies, University of Hong Kong. 212 pages.

Shifting Paradigms and Asian Perspectives: Implications for Research and Teaching. Research Paper Series, No. 10. Centre for Advanced Studies, National University of Singapore. 22 pages.

Hong Kong: After Smooth Handover, now the Hard Part (with John

Wong). Singapore: East Asian Institute Background Briefs, 1999.

"Chineseness: the Dilemmas of Place and Practice". In *Cosmopolitan Capitalists: Hong Kong and the Chinese Diaspora at the end of the 20th Century*. Edited by Gary Hamilton. Seattle: University of Washington Press, pp. 118–134.

"A Single Chinese Diaspora? Some Historical Reflections." In *Imagining the Chinese Diaspora: Two Australian Perspectives*. Canberra: Centre for the Study of the Chinese Southern Diaspora, pp. 1–17.

"ASEAN and the Three Powers of the Asia-Pacific". In *Southeast Asia's Changing Landscape: Implications for U.S.-Japan Relations on the Eve of the Twenty-First Century*. Edited by Gerrit W. Gong. Washington, D.C.: The Center for Strategic and International Studies, pp. 19–26.

"Education and Bridging Work Cultures" (The 2nd Asa Briggs Lecture). *Forum on Open Learning: Empowerment through Knowledge and Technology*. Brunei: The Commonwealth of Learning and University of Brunei Darussalam, March 1999 (http://www.col.org/forum/wang.htm)

"Openness and Nationalism: Outside the Chinese Revolution", translated into Spanish and published in *El nacionalismo chino* (Barcelona: Bellaterra Publishers, 1999).

[First published in *Chinese Nationalism*, edited by Jonathan Unger, Armonk, NY: M.E. Sharpe, pp. 113–125.]

"Minzu zhuyi, zhongzu xin yu Yatai quyue 民族主义，种族心性与亚太区域", *Zhongguo Shehui kexue jikan* (Chinese Social Sciences Quarterly), Hong Kong, No. 25, pp. 17–30.

"Danyi di huaren sanjuzhe? 单一的华人散居者?" (A Single Chinese Diaspora?), *Huaqiao huaren lishi yanjiu* (Beijing), no. 3, September, pp. 1–17.

"Zhongguo zai Yatai quyue di diwei: xunqiu mengyou he pengyou 中国在亚太区域的地位: 寻求盟友和朋友" (China's Place in the Region), *Yazhou Pinglun* (Asian Review), No. 9, pp. 69–80.

"Qiaoxiang Ties: 'Cultural Capitalism' in South China (Preface)".

In *Qiaoxiang Ties: Interdisciplinary Approaches to 'Cultural Capitalism' in South China*. Edited by Leo Douw, Cen Huang and Michael R. Godley. London and Leiden: Kegan Paul International and International Institute for Asian Studies, pp. 1–2.

2000

The Chinese Overseas: From Earthbound China to the Quest for Autonomy. Cambridge, MA: Harvard University Press. 148 pages. (Paperback edition published in 2002.)

Joining the Modern World: Inside and Outside China. Singapore: University of Singapore Press and World Scientific Publishing. 159 pages.

Tandang rensheng, xuezhe qinghuai: Wang Gengwu fangtan yu yanlunji. 坦荡人生, 学者情怀·王赓武访谈与言论集. Edited by Liu Hong. River Edge, N.J.: Global Publishing Co. 275 pages.

Reform, Legitimacy and Dilemmas: China's Politics and Society (Editor, with Zheng Yongnian). Singapore: University of Singapore Press and World Scientific Publishing. 375 pages.

"Ethnic Chinese: The Past in their Future". In Teresita Ang See (ed.) *Intercultural Relations, Cultural Transformation, and Identity — The Ethnic Chinese* (Selected Papers presented at the 1998 ISSCO Conference). Manila: Kaisa Para Sa Kaunlaran, Manila, 2000, pp. 1–20.

[Also published in *Chinese America: History and Perspectives 2000*. San Francisco: Chinese Historical Society of America and San Francisco State University, 2000, pp. 1–9.]

[Chinese translation by Qian Jiang, "Cong lishi zhong xunqiu weilaidi haiwai huaren 从历史中寻求未来地海外华人", *Huaqiao huaren lishi yanjiu 华侨华人历史研究*, Beijing, no. 4, 1999, pp. 1–11]

[Indonesian translation by Ignatius Wibowo, "Orang etnis Cina menchari sejarah". In *Harga yang Harus Dibayar: Sketsa Pergaulatan Etnis Cina di Indonesia*. Edited by Ignatius Wibowo. Jakarta: Penerbit PT Gramedia Pustaka Utama, pp. 1–34.]

"Memories of War: World War II in Asia". In P. Lim Pui Huen and Diana Wong, eds., *War and Memory in Malaysia and Singapore.* Singapore: Institute of Southeast Asian Studies. pp. 11–22.

"Questions of Identity during the Qing Dynasty", In *Proceedings of the 3rd Conference on Sinology*, Taipei: Academia Sinica and National Science Council, 2002.

"Joining the Modern World". In Wang Gungwu, *Joining the Modern World*, pp. 1–14.

"The Chinese Revolution and the Overseas Chinese". In Wang Gungwu, *Joining the Modern World,* pp. 15–36.

"Hong Kong and an Ambivalent Modernity". In Wang Gungwu, *Joining the Modern World,* pp. 71–82.

"The Shanghai–Hong Kong Linkage", In Wang Gungwu, *Joining the Modern World*, pp. 83–95.

"Transforming the Trading Chinese", In Wang Gungwu, *Joining the Modern World*, pp. 97–106.

"Chinese Values and Memories of Modern War". In Wang Gungwu, *Joining the Modern World*, pp. 107–128.

"Modern Work Cultures and the Chinese". In Wang Gungwu, *Joining the Modern World*, pp. 129–149.

"Introduction"; and "Les Chinois de la diaspora et le nationalisme". In *Encyclopedie de la Diaspora Chinese.* Edited by Lynn Pan (French edition). Paris: Les Editions du Pacifique, pp. 10–13; 103–105.

"Huaren yimin bianqian shi 华人移民变迁史 (Changes in Chinese migration history)". In Rao Meijiao, Guo Yiyao and Zheng Cheyan, eds. *Yishi E'e − Huang Shihua xiansheng 'Ba-yi' rongshou zhengwen ji − 士谔谔: 黄石华先生《八一》荣寿征文集.* Hong Kong; Huixin Publishers, pp. 225–246.

Ershi nianqian de yiduan wangshi – Wang Gengwu xiaozhang tan 'Nanda shijian' 二十年前的一段往事 − 王赓武校长谈'南大事件'. In 刘宏 (主编). *坦荡人生, 学者情怀: 王赓武访谈与言论集 Tandang rensheng, xuezhe qinghuai: Wang Gengwu fangtan yu yanlunji.* Edited by Liu Hong. River Edge, N.J.: Global Publishing Co. 2000, pp. 38–47.

(Originally published in *Xueyuan* 学苑, HKU Students' Society 香港大学学生会, 1986). Republished in Li Yelin, ed. *Nanyang Daxue zouguo di lishi daolu* 南洋大学走过的历史道路. Petaling Jaya: Malaiya Nanyang Daxue Xiaoyouhui (Nanyang University Alumni Association of Malaya), 2002, pp. 391–396.)

"Political Heritage and Nation Building", *Journal of the Malaysian Branch of the Royal Asiatic Society*, Kuala Lumpur, vol. LXIII, part 2, pp. 5–30.

2001

Only Connect! Sino-Malay Encounters. Singapore: Times Academic Press. 304 pages. (Republished, Singapore: Eastern Universities Press, 2003.)

Don't Leave Home: Migration and the Chinese. Singapore: Times Academic Press. 320 pages. (Republished, Singapore: Eastern Universities Press, 2003.)

"Continuities in Island Southeast Asia". In *Reinventing Malaysia: Reflections on its Past and Future*. Edited by Jomo, K.S. Bangi, Malaysia: Penerbit Universiti Kebangsaan Malaysia, pp. 15–34.

"Reflections on Networks and Structures in Asia". In *Asianizing Asia: Reflexivity, History and Identity*. *B*angkok: Asian Studies in Asia Foundation, pp. 15–32.

"Europe's Heritage in Asia". In *Asia-Europe on the Eve of the 21st Century*. Edited by Suthiphand Chirathivat, Franz Knipping, Poul-Henrik Lassen and Chia Siow Yue. Bangkok & Singapore: Centre for European Studies at Chulalongkorn University and Institute of Southeast Asian Studies, pp. 17–27.

"Zhongguo renkou qianyi: guoqu yu xianzai 中国人口迁移过去与现在 (People movement in China, past and present)". In *Ershiyi shiji: wenhua zijue yu kuawenhua duihua* 二十一世纪: 文化自觉与跨文化对话 (21st Century: cultural self-consciousness and cross-cultural dialogue). Vol. One. Edited by Ma Rong and Zhou Xing. Beijing: Peking University Press, pp. 273–289.

"Shifting paradigms and Asian Perspectives: Implications for research and teaching". In *Reflections on Alternative Discourses from Southeast Asia*. Edited by Syed Farid Alatas. Singapore: Pagesetters Services, pp. 47–54.

"The Search for National Histories", *Asian Culture* (Yazhou wenhua), Singapore, no. 25, pp. 1–14.

(An earlier version appeared in *Southeast Asian Area Studies, Academia Sinica, Newsletter*, Taipei, No. 11, 2000, pp. 124–138.)

"Diaspora, a much abused word" (Interview by Editor). *Asian Affairs*, Hong Kong, no. 14, winter, pp. 17–29.

"Transforming the Trading World of Southeast Asia", in e-journal, *The Asianists' Asia*, Centre de Recherche sur les Etudes Asiatiques, Paris, pp. 60-65. *(http://hometown.aol.com/wignesh).*

"Xin yimin: heyi xin? weihe xin? 新移民: 何以新? 为何新?" (New migrants: How new? Why new?), Translated by Cheng Xi. *Huaqiao huaren lishi yanjiu* (Overseas Chinese History Studies), Beijing, no. 4, pp. 1–8.

"The Future of Secular Values", Electronic edition of the Social Science Research Council (New York) Papers on "After September 11", 31 October, 2001. *(http://www.ssrc.org/sept11/essays/wang.htm)*

2002

To Act is to Know: Chinese Dilemmas. Singapore: Times Academic Press. 321 pages. (Republished, Singapore: Eastern Universities Press, 2003)

Bind Us in Time: Nation and civilisation in Asia. Singapore: Times Academic Press. 306 pages. (Republished, Singapore: Eastern Universities Press, 2003)

Haiwai huaren yanjiu di dashiye yu xinfangxiang: Wang Gengwu jiaoshou lunwenji 海外华人研究的大视野与新方向; 王赓武教授论文集. Edited by Liu Hong and Huang Jianli. River Edge, NJ: Global Publishing. 436 pages.

Wang Gengwu Zixuanji 王赓武自选集 (Selected Works). Shanghai: Shanghai Education Press. 325 pages.

Wang Fo-wen jinianji 王宓文纪念集 (Wang Fo-wen, 1903–1972: a memorial collection of poems, essays and calligraphy). River Edge, N.J: Bafang wenhua Global Publishing. xlix + 124 pages (173 pages).

"State and Faith: Secular Values in Asia and the West". In Eric Herschberg and Kevin W. Moore (eds.), *Critical Views of September 11: Analyses from around the world*. New York: The New Press, pp. 224–242.

"Local and National: a dialogue between tradition and modernity". In Leo Suryadinata (ed.), *Ethnic Chinese in Singapore and Malaysia: A Dialogue between Tradition and Modernity*. Singapore: Times Academic Press, 2002, pp. 1–8.

"Haiwai huaren di wenhua zhongxin 海外华人的文化中心". In Hao Shiyuan 郝时远 (ed.) *Haiwai huaren lunji* 海外华人论集 (Essays on Chinese Overseas). Translated by Zhang Haiyang. Beijing: Chinese Academy of Social Sciences Press, pp. 211–230.

"Zailun haiwai huaren di shenfen rentong 再论海外华人的身份认同" (Chinese identity revisited). In Li Zhuoran, ed., *Hanxue zongheng* 汉学纵横 (Excursions in Sinology). Hong Kong: Commercial Press, pp. 45–63.

"New migrants: How new? Why new?" In Chang Tsun-wu and Tang Shi-yeoung (eds.) *Hai-wai hua-tsu yen-chiu lun-ji.* (Essays on Ethnic Chinese Abroad). Three Volumes. Vol. I: Migration, Entrepreneurs and Commerce. Taipei: Overseas Chinese Association, pp. i–xi.

"Haiwai huaren yu zuowei zhongguo ren 海外华人与作为中国人". In *Huaqiao huaren baike quanshu* 华侨华人百科全书 (Encyclopedia of Chinese Overseas), in 12 volumes. Vol. 1: General Studies, Beijing: Chinese Overseas Publishing House, 2002, pp. 42–49.

"City, and Citadel, on the Hill", [in One Year On: Power, Purpose and Strategy in American Foreign Policy], *The National Interest*, no. 69, pp. 23–26.

"China and Southeast Asia: collision or co-operation?" *Trends in Southeast Asia*, Singapore, No. 3, February, pp. 12–21.

"Globalization and Human Civilization", *Journal of Nanjing University (Natural Sciences)*, vol. 38, Special Issue for World Scientists Forum, November, pp. 132–140.

2003

Anglo-Chinese Encounters since 1800: War, Trade, Science and Governance. Cambridge: Cambridge University Press. 202 pages.

Hwa Kyo (The Chinese Overseas) [The Chinese Overseas; From Earthbound China to the Quest for Autonomy]. Translated by Yun Pil-Chun. Seoul: Darakwon Publishing Co. 2003. 155 pages.

Ideas Won't Keep: the struggle for China's future. Singapore: Eastern Universities Press. 249 pages.

Power and Identity in the Chinese World Order: Festschrift in Honour of Professor Wang Gungwu. Edited by Billy K.L. So, John Fitzgerald, Huang Jianli and James K. Chin. Hong Kong: Hong Kong University Press. 460 pages.

China and the Chinese Overseas. Re-published. Singapore: Eastern Universities Press. 352 pages.

Damage Control: the Chinese Communist Party in the Era of Jiang Zeming (Editor, with Zheng Yongnian). Singapore: Eastern Universities Press. 383 pages.

Sino-Asiatica: Papers dedicated to Professor Liu Ts'un-yan on the occasion of his eighty-fifth birthday. (Editor, with Rafe de Crespigny and Igor de Rachewiltz). Canberra: Faculty of Asian Studies, ANU. 241 pages.

The Iraq War and its Consequences: Thoughts of Nobel Laureates and Eminent Scholars (Editor, with Irwin Abrams). Singapore: World Scientific, 443 pages.

Yizhan qishilu 伊战启示录 (Iraq: an Unveiling). (Editor, with Gong Shaopeng 龚少鹏). Singapore: Bafang wenhua Publishers. 221 pages.

The Chinese Diaspora: Selected Essays. (Editor, with Wang Ling-chi) Two volumes. Republished. Singapore: Eastern Universities Press. Vol. 1, 375 pages; Vol. 2, 399 pages.

"Social Bonding and Freedom: Problems of Choice in Immigrant Societies". In Michael W. Charney, Brenda S.A. Yeoh and Tong Chee Kiong (eds.), *Asian Migrants and Education: the tensions of education in Immigrant Societies and among migrant groups*. Dordrecht and Boston: Kluwer Academic Publishers, pp. 1–13.

"Chinese Political Culture and Scholarship about the Malay World". In Ding Choo Ming (ed.) *Chinese Scholarship on the Malay World: a revaluation of a scholarly tradition*. Singapore: Eastern Universities Press, pp. 1–30.

"Reflections on Networks and Structures in Asia". In Melissa G. Curley and Liu Hong (eds), *China and Southeast Asia: changing social-cultural interactions*. Hong Kong: Hong Kong University Centre of Asian Studies, pp. 13–26.

"Questions of Identity during the Ch'ing Dynasty". In Jiang Bin and He Cuiping (eds.) *Guojia, shichang yu molohua de zuqun* 国家、市场与脉咯化的族群. *Proceedings of the Third International Sinology Conference: Anthropology*. In Two volumes. Taipei: Academia Sinica, Volume1, pp. 31–58.

"The Limits of Decolonization". In Marc Frey, Ronald W. Preussen and Tan Tay Yong (eds.), *The Transformation of Southeast Asia: International Perspectives on Decolonization*. Armonk, N.Y.: M.E. Sharpe, pp. 268–273.

"The Travails of National Confucianism". In Wang Gungwu, Rafe de Crespigny and Igor de Rachewiltz (eds.), *Sino-Asiatica: Papers dedicated to Professor Liu Ts'un-yan on the occasion of his eighty-fifth birthday*. Canberra: Faculty of Asian Studies, ANU, pp. 212–237.

"Jiaozhizhu huiyi yu kewang: yiminzhouqi de zuishuo 交織著回憶與渴望: 移民週期的追溯 (Mixing Memory and Desire: Tracking the Migrant Cycle)". (Translated by 邱淑如 (Ann Chiu Shu-ju). In Conference Proceedings, Second Conference on Chinese Overseas: Research and Documentation. 第二屆海外華人研究與文獻收藏機構國際會議論文集 (Electronic edition). Chinese University of Hong Kong, March 2003, 10 pages.)

"China Rising: prospects and implications for Asia Pacific". In Elina Noor and Mohamed Jawhar Hassan (eds.), *Asia Pacific Security: Uncertainty in a Changing World Order*, Kuala Lumpur: Institute of Strategic and International Studies, 2003, pp. 279–285.

"Prospects for Pacific Asia Integration" (with Jesus P. Estanislao). In *Global Governance: Enhancing Trilateral Cooperation*, Seoul: The Trilateral Commission, 2003, pp. 49–60.

"Auslandchinesen (The Chinese Overseas)". In Brunhild Staiger, Stefan Freidrich and Hans-Wilm Schutte (eds.) *Das grosse China-Lexikon*. Darmstadt: Wissenschaftliche Buchgeselleschaft, pp. 37–42.

"Minzu zhuyi yu Rujia xueshuo 民族主义与儒家学说 (Nationalism and Confucianism)". In Chen Rongzhao, Ed. *Ruxue yu Shijie Wenming: guoji xueshu huiyi lunwen xuanji 儒学与世界文明: 国际学术会议论文选集* (Confucianism and World Civilization). Two vols. Singapore: National University of Singapore Department of Chinese Studies and Global Publishing Co., vol. 1, pp. 37–44.

"Who Should Pay for Universities?" In K.K. Phua, Hew Choy Sin and Ong Choon Nam, eds. *The Tan Kah Kee Spirit Today*. Singapore: Tan Kah Kee Foundation & Tan Kah Kee International Society, pp. 45–73.

"Wang Gungwu: An Oral History" (by Lee Guan-kin). In Billy K.L. So, John Fitzgerald, Huang Jianli and James K. Chin (eds.) *Power and Identity in the Chinese World Order: Festschrift in Honour of Professor Wang Gungwu*. Hong Kong: Hong Kong University Press, pp. 375–427.

"Secular China" (Giri Deshingkar Memorial Lecture), *China Report*, vol. 39, no. 3, July–September 2003, pp. 305–321.

"Overseas Chinese & Ethnic Chinese Studies: methodologies" (with Shiba Yoshinobu, Hamashita Takeshi, Chen Tianxi and Takahashi Goro), *China 21*, vol. 17, November, pp. 3–26.

"Asian Civilisations...Future Frontiers". Report on "Many Chinas: Cultural Difference and Political Unity", 20 June 2003. (*http://www.siiaonline.org/article/Wang%20Gungwu.pdf*)

2004

Diasporic Chinese ventures: The Life and Work of Wang Gungwu. Edited by Gregor Benton and Liu Hong. London: RoutledgeCurzon. 246 pages

Maritime China in Transition, 1750–1850. (Editor, with Ng Chin-keong). Wiesbaden: Harrassowitz Verlag, 397 pages.

Global History and Migrations. Republished. Newton Center, MA: New Global History Press, 2004.

What Asia Understands of U.S. Grand Strategy (Asian Voices Series, December 2003). Washington, D.C.: Sasakawa Peace Foundation, 2004. 28 pages.

"Maritime China in Transition". In Wang Gungwu and Ng Chin-keong (eds.) *Maritime China in Transition, 1750–1850*. Wiesbaden: Harrassowitz Verlag, pp. 3–16.

"China's Long Road to Sovereignty". In G. Doeker-Mach and K.A. Ziegert (eds.) *Law and Legal Culture*. Stuttgart: Franz Steiner Verlag, 2004, pp. 453–464.

"Cultural Centres for the Chinese Overseas". In Wong Siu-lun and Melissa Curley (eds.), *Chinese and Indian Diasporas: Comparative Perspectives*. Hong Kong: Centre of Asian Studies, University of Hong Kong, 2004, pp. 27–50.

"Chinese Ethnicity in New Southeast Asian Nations". In Leo Suryadinata (ed.) *Ethnic Relations and Nation-building in Southeast Asia: The Case of the Ethnic Chinese*. Singapore: Institute of Southeast Asian Studies, 2004, pp. 1–19.

"The Uses of Dynastic Ideology: Confucianism in Contemporary Business". In Frank-Jurgen Richter and Pamela C.M. Mar (eds.), *Asia's New Crisis: Renewal though Total Ethical Management*. Singapore" John Wiley & Sons (Asia) Pte Ltd, 2004, pp. 51–62.

"China between Progress and Tradition". In Shan Zhouyao, Li Zhuoran and Wang Runhua (eds.) *East-West Studies: Tradition, Transformation and Innovation. A Festschrift in Honour of Professor Chiu Ling Yeong on his Retirement* [Dongxi wenhua chengchuan yu chuangxing: Zhao Lingyang jiaoshou rongxiu

jinian lunwenji 东西文化承传与创新: 赵令扬教授荣休纪
念论文集]. Singapore: Bafang wenhua and Uni Press, 2004,
pp. 3–9.

"The Cultural Implications of the Rise of China for the Region". In
Kokubun Ryosei and Wang Jisi (eds.), *The Rise of China and a
Changing East Asian Order*. Tokyo and New York: Japan Center
for International Exchange, 2004. pp. 77–87.

"The Search for Asian National Histories". In Ahmat Adam and
Lai Yew Meng (eds.), *IAHA 2000: Proceedings of the 16th
Conference of the International Association of Historians of
Asia*, Volume I, Kota Kinabalu: Universiti Malaysia Sabah,
2004, pp. 275–283.

"Closing Comments and Questions". In C.C. Chin and Karl Hack
(eds.), *Dialogues with Chin Peng: New Light on the Malayan
Communist Party*. Singapore: Singapore University Press, 2004,
pp. 225–242.

"Cong Chen Jaigeng jingshen dao Nanda jingshen — zoufang Wang
Gengwu jiaoshou 从陈嘉庚精神到南大精神 — 走访王赓武
教授" (From Tan Kah Kee Spirit to the Spirit of Nanyang
University), In *Nanda Jingshen 南大精神* (edited by the Editorial
Group of Tan Kah Kee International Society), Singapore:
Bafang Wenhua and Tan Kah Kee International Society, 2003,
pp. 21–27.

"The Fourth Rise of China: Cultural Implications", *China: An
International Journal*, Vol. 2, No. 2, September 2004,
pp. 311–322.

"Cultures Today and the Chinese Heritage" and "Xiandai wenhua
yu Huaren chuantong 现代文化与华人传统", *CHC Bulletin
— Huayiguan tongxun*. No. 3, June 2004, pp. 6–19.

"Perspectives of United States Grand Strategy in a Changing
Southeast Asia", *Yazhou wenhua (Asian Culture)*. No. 28, 2004,
pp. 27–39.

"Wuyi jietuo di kunjing? 无以解脱的困境? (Writing as *haiwai huaren*:
Dilemma without Relief?)", *Dushu 读书* (Beijing). 10/2004,
pp. 110–120.

"The Age of New Paradigms" (Keynote Lecture, 18th Conference of International Association of Historians of Asia, December 2004), *Yatai yanjiu luntan* 亚太研究论坛 (Asia-Pacific Forum), no. 26, 2004, pp. 1–15.

"New Developments in Southeast Asian Studies", *Yatai yanjiu luntan* 亚太研究论坛 (Asia Pacific Forum), no. 23, 2004.

"2003 in Review", *Singapore Yearbook 2004*. Singapore: National Archives of Singapore, pp. 6–11.

2005

Yimin ji xingqi de Zhongguo 移民及兴起的中国 (Migrants and China's Rise). River Edge, N.J. and Singapore: Global Publishing, Bafang wenhua qiye, 2005.

Nation-building: Five Southeast Asian Histories. (Editor). Singapore: Institute of Southeast Asian Studies, 2005. 288 pages.

The Universal and the Historical: My Faith in History. (Daisaku Ikeda Annual Lecture, 2004). Singapore: Singapore Soka Association, 2005, 20 pages.

"China and Southeast Asia". In David Shambaugh (ed.) *Power Shift: China and Asia's New Dynamics*. Berkeley: University of California Press, 2005. pp. 187–204.

"Two Perspectives of Southeast Asian Studies: Singapore and China" and "Preface". In Paul H. Kratoska, Remco Rabin and Henk Schulte Nordholt (eds.), *Locating Southeast Asia: Genealogies of Knowledge and Politics of Space*. Singapore and Athens, OH: Singapore University Press and Ohio University Press, 2005, pp. 60–81 and x–xi.

"Haiwai huaren yanzhongdi Zhongguo bianqian 海外华人眼中的中国变迁" (Change in China in the eyes of the Chinese Abroad). In Xu Jilin and Liu Qing (eds.), *Liwa hepan lun sixiang — Huadong Shifan daxue siyuwen jiangzuo yanjianglu 丽娃河畔论思想 — 华东师范大学思与文讲座演讲录* (Discussing Ideas by the Liwa River: Lectures on Thought and Literature at East China Normal University). Shanghai: Huadong shifan daxue Press, 2005, pp. 341–347.

"China and Southeast Asia: Changes in Strategic Perceptions". In Ho Khai Leong and Samuel C.Y. Ku (eds.) *China and Southeast Asia: Global Changes and Regional Challenges.* Singapore and Kaohsiung: Institute of Southeast Asian Studies and National Sun Yat-sen University Center for Southeast Asian Studies, 2005, pp. 3–14.

"Migration and its Enemies". In Bruce Mazlish and Akira Iriye (Eds.), *The Global History Reader*, New York: Routledge, 2005, pp. 104–113. (Originally published in 1993.)

"The Opening of Relations between China and Malacca, 1403–05" and "The First Three Rulers of Malacca". In Leo Suryadinata (ed.), *Admiral Zheng He and Southeast Asia.* Singapore International Zheng He Society and Institute of Southeast Asian Studies, 2005, pp. 1–25, 26–41. (Originally published in 1964 and 1968.)

"A New Sensation", in *Twenty-two Malaysian Stories: an anthology of writing in English.* Selected and edited by Lloyd Fernando. Petaling Jaya: Maya Press, pp. 117–131. New edition of collection first published in Singapore: Heinemann Educational Books (Asia), pp. 113–125.

"Within and Without: Chinese Writers Overseas", *Journal of Chinese Overseas*, vol. 1, no. 1 (May 2005), pp. 1–15.

"Shangyezhong di Rujia lunli? 商业中的儒家伦理? (Confucian Ethics in Business?)", *Chinese Cross Currents (Shenzhou jiaoliu 神州 交流*), vol. 2, no. 2, 2005, pp. 9–19.

2006

"Inception, Origins, Contemplations: a Personal Perspective". In *Imagination, Openness & Courage: The National University of Singapore at 100.* Singapore: National University of Singapore, 2006, pp. 1–31.

"Lishi yu zhishi: zhongxi fenlei de chayi (历史与知识: 中西分类的 差异, History and Knowledge: different library classifications in China and the West)". In 《庆祝钱存训教授九五华诞学术论 文集》编辑委员会编, *Nanshan lunxueji: Qian Cunxun xiansheng*

jiuwu shengri jinian (南山论学集: 钱存训先生九五生日纪念).
Beijing: Beijing tushuguan, 2006, pp. 24–30.

"Chinese Ethnicity in New Southeast Asian Nations". In Lee Guan Kin (editor), *Demarcating Ethnicity in New Nations: Cases of the Chinese in Singapore, Malaysia, and Indonesia.* Singapore: Singapore Society of Asian studies and Konrad Adenauer Stiftung, 2006, pp. 19–35.

"Patterns of Chinese Migration in historical perspective"; "The Study of Chinese Minorities in Southeast Asia"; "Greater China and the Chinese Overseas"; "Political Chinese: their contribution to modern Southeast Asian history", and "Foreword". Collected in Liu Hong (ed.) *The Chinese Overseas* (Routledge Library of Modern China). Oxford: Routledge, in four volumes, 2006, pp. xv–xviii; vol. I, pp. 33–49; 258–278; 432–456; vol. IV, 163–176.

"Some Remarks on Singapore and Asia in this Era of Globalisation". In Lai Ah Eng (editor), *Going Glocal: Being Singaporean in a Globalised World* (Singapore Perspectives 2006). Singapore: Institute of Policy Studies and Marshall Cavendish, 2006, pp. 133–140.

"People and the Coombs Effect". In Brij Lal and Allison Ley (eds.), *The Coombs: A House of Memories.* Canberra: Research School of Pacific and Asian Studies, 2006, pp. 43–46.

"Zhongguo wenhua haiwaiguan 中国文化海外观 (Chinese Culture from Outside China)", 西安交通大学学报 (社会科学版) Journal of Xi'an Jiaotong University (Social Sciences), vol. 27, no. 81, 1/2007, pp. 1–5.

2007

Divided China: Preparing for reunification, 883–947. Second Revised Edition of *The Structure of Power in North China during the Five Dynasties* (First Edition, 1963). Singapore: World Scientific Publishing Co., 2007. 224 pages.

Lixiang bietu: jingwai kanzhonghua 离乡别土: 境外看中华 (China and Its Cultures: From the Periphery). The Fu Ssu-nien Memorial

Lectures 2005. Taipei: Institute of History and Philology, Academia Sinica, 2007. 86 pages.

Chuka Bunmei to Chugoku no yukue 中华文明と中国のゆくえ (Chinese Civilization and China's Position).The Ishizaka 石坂 Lectures 2005. Translated into Japanese by Kato Mikio 加藤 幹雄. Tokyo: Iwanami Shoten, 2007. 181 pages.

"The First Decade: Historical Perspectives". In *The First Decade: The Hong Kong SAR in Retrospective and Introspective Perspectives*. Edited by Yeung Yue-man. Hong Kong: The Chinese University Press, 2007, pp. 3–21.

"Trading Order and Polity Structures in Asia". In *The Inclusive Regionalist: A Festschrift dedicated to Jusuf Wanandi*. Edited by Hadi Soesastro and Clara Joewono. Jakarta: Centre for Strategic and International Studies (CSIS), 2007, pp. 83–90.

"*Liuxue* 留学 and *yimin* 移民: From Study to Migranthood". In *Beyond Chinatown: New Chinese Migration and the Global Expansion of China*. Edited by Mette Thuno. Copenhagen: NIAS Press, 2007. pp. 165–181.

"The Rise of China: History as Policy". In *History as Policy: Framing the Debate on the Future of Australia's Defence Policy*. Canberra: epressanu.edu.au (Australian National University Strategic and Defence Studies Centre's 40th Anniversary Series), 2007, pp. 61–66.

"Mixing Memory and Desire: Tracking the Migrant Cycles". In *Chinese Overseas: Migration, Research and Documentation*. Edited by Tan Chee-Beng, Colin Storey and Julia Zimmerman. Hong Kong: Chinese University Press, 2007, pp. 3–22.

"The Pull of Southeast Asia". In *Historians and Their Disciplines: the Call of Southeast Asian History*. Edited by Nicholas Tarling. Kuala Lumpur: MBRAS Monograph No. 40, 2007, pp. 161–174.

"China: Economic Strength and Structural Weaknesses?" In *7th Asian-European Editors' Forum*. Edited by Werner vom Busch and Tobias Rettig. Singapore: Konrad-Adenauer-Stiftung, 2007, pp. 17–27.

"The Nanhai Trade: A Study of the Early History of Chinese Trade in the South China Sea" and "The First Three Rulers of Malacca". In *Southeast Asia-China Interactions: Reprint of Articles from Journal of the Malaysian Branch of the Royal Asiatic Society.* Edited by Geoff Wade. Reprint no. 25. Kuala Lumpur: MBRAS, 2007, pp. 51–166; 317–326.

"Rethinking Chinese History in a global Age: an Interview with Wang Gungwu" by Alan Baumler, *The Chinese Historical Review*, vol. 14, no. 1, Spring 2007, pp. 97–113.

"In Conversation with Wang Gungwu" by Vineeta Sinha, *ISA (International Sociological Association) E-Bulletin*, no. 6, March 2007, pp. 54–80.

"The Great Powers in Asia: a View from Singapore", *Strategy: Global Forces 2007 Proceedings*, vol. 2. Canberra: Australian Strategic Policy Institute, December 2007, pp. 1–8.

"The Age of Paradigms", *ISA (International Sociological Association) E-Bulletin*, no. 6, March 2007, pp. 80–100. (First published in 2004.)

"Zouxiang xin de xiandaixing: xianggang huigui de lishishijiao 走向新的现代性: 香港回归的历史视角" (Towards New Modernity: The Return of Hong Kong from a Historical Perspective), 二十一世纪 *(Twenty-First Century)*, no. 101, June 2007, pp. 4–12.

2008

China and the New International Order. (Editor, with Zheng Yongnian). London: Routledge, 2008. 316 pages.

"The China Seas: Becoming an Enlarged Mediterranean", In Angela Schottenhammer (Ed.), *The East Asian 'Mediterranean': Maritime Crossroads of Culture, Commerce ad Human Migration.* Wiesbaden: Harrassowitz Verlag. 2008, pp. 7–22.

"Flag, Flame and Embers: Diaspora Cultures". In Kam Louie (Ed.), *The Cambridge Companion to Modern Chinese Cultures*. Cambridge: Cambridge University Press, 2008, pp. 115–134.

"China and the International Order: Some Historical Perspectives". In

Wang Gungwu and Zheng Yongnian (eds), *China and the New International Order*. London: Routledge, 2008, pp. 21–31.

"南侨求学记: 不同的时代, 走不同的路 (In Search of Learning: Different Times, Different Roads". In 李元瑾 Lee Guan Kin (Ed.), *跨越疆界与文化调适*. 南洋理工大学中华语言文化中心; 八方文化创作室, 2008, pp. 13–28.

"Nei yu wai de jiexi — lun haiwai huaren zuojia 内与外的解析 — 论海外华人作家" (Translation of "Within and Without: Chinese Writers Overseas"), *世界华侨华人研究 Overseas Chinese Studies*. Vol. 1, 2008, pp. 1–10.

"A note on the Origins of *Hua-ch'iao*". In Anthony Reid (ed.), *The Chinese Diaspora in the Pacific*. Aldershot, Hants: Ashgate, 2008. (First published in 1977.)

"前所未有的感觉 (A New Sensation)" [by Awang Kedua] (Translation by Hu Bao-zhu 胡寶珠). In 张锦忠、黄锦树、庄华兴 (编)。回到马来亚：华马小说七十年。*Return to Malaya: Stories by Chinese Malaysian Writiers, 1937–2007* (Edited by Tee Kim Tong, Ng Kim Chew and Chong Fah Hing). Batu Caves, Selangor: 大将出版社 Mentor Publishing, 2008, pp. 51–61.

2009

Zhongguo de 'zhuyi' zhi zheng — cong 'wusiyundong' dao dangdai 中国的《主义》之争 — 从《五四运动》到当代. (China's Ideological Battles since the May Fourth Movement (Editor, with Zheng Yongnian). 新加坡: 八方文化创作室。Singapore: World Scientific Publishing, 2009. 381 pages.

Voice of Malayan Revolution: The CPM Radio War against Singapore and Malaysia, 1960–1981 (Editor, with Ong Weichong). Singapore: S. Rajaratnam School of International Studies, 2009. 350 pages.

Hong Kong Challenge: Leaning In and Facing Out. Hong Kong: University of Hong Kong Centre of Asian Studies Hong Kong Culture & Society Occasional Paper Series, 2009, no. 8. 12 pages.

"Family and Friends: China in Changing Asia". In Anthony Reid and

Zheng Yangwen (eds.) *Negotiating Asymmetry: China's Place in Asia*. Singapore: NUS Press, 2009, pp. 214–231.

"The Fifty Years Before". In Peter H.L. Lim (ed.) *1959–2009: Chronicle of Singapore: Fifty Years of Headline News*. Singapore: Editions Didier Millet and National Library Board, 2009, pp. 15–27.

"One Country, Two Cultures: An Alternative View of Hong Kong". In Elizabeth Sinn, Wong Siu-lun and Chan Wing-hoi (eds.), *Rethinking Hong Kong: New Paradigms, New Perspectives*. Hong Kong: Centre of Asian Studies, University of Hong Kong, 2009, pp. 1–24.

"Plus One", "Three Faces of Night" and "A New Sensation", In Angelia Poon, Philip Holden & Shirley Geok-lin Lim (eds.), *Writing Singapore: An Historical Anthology of Singapore Literature*. Singapore: NUS Press and National Arts Council, 2009, pp. 106–117.

"Chinese History Paradigms", *Asian Ethnicity*, vol. 10, no. 3, October 2009, pp. 201–216.

"Yueyang xunqiu kongjian: zhongguo de yimin 越洋寻求空间: 中国的移民" (Seeking their own space: China's Migrants), 华人研究国际学报 *International Journal of Diasporic Chinese Studies*, vol. 1, no. 1, 2009, pp. 1–49.

"Southeast Asia: Imperial themes", *New Zealand Journal of Asian Studies*, June, 2009, pp. 36–48.

2010

"Dangguo minzhu: sandai haiwai huaren de jin yu tui 黨國民主: 三代海外華人的進與退" (Party-state democracy: Three Generations of Chinese overseas), 中央研究院近代史研究所集刊, Bulletin no. 67, 2010, pp. 1–15 [Also published in 僑協雜誌 *OCA Bimonthly Magazine*, no. 121, Mar–Apr, 2010, pp. 4–15.]

"The Peranakan Phenomenon: Pre-national, Marginal, and Transnational". In Leo Suryadinata (Editor). *Peranakan Chinese in a Globalizing Southeast Asia*. Singapore: Chinese Heritage Centre and National University of Singapore Museum Baba House, 2010, pp. 14–26.

"Post-imperial Knowledge and Pre-Social Science in Southeast Asia". In Goh Beng-Lan (Editor). *Decentring and Diversifying Southeast Asian Studies: Perspectives from the Region.* Singapore: Institute of Southeast Asian Studies, 2010.

Index

With his parents in Ipoh, 1934

Age 6, at his grandfather's home in Taizhou, Jiangsu

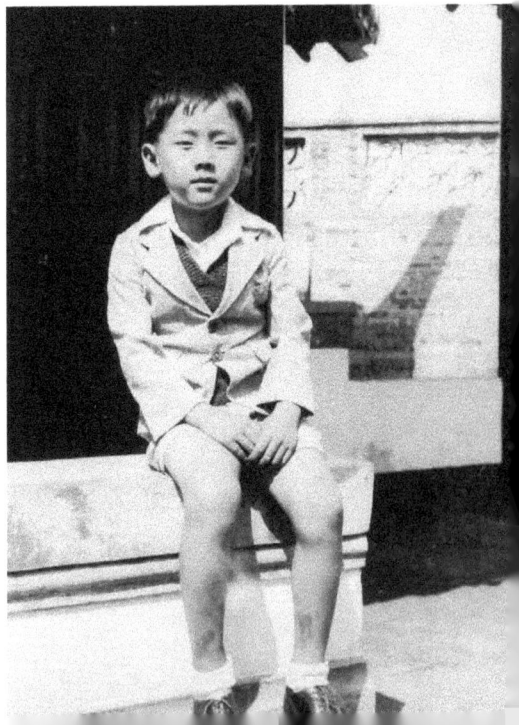

Nanjing, late 1947

Back row, left corner, beside his father, his mother between them, with his grandfather (in black robe) in Taizhou, 1948

Hosting an exhibition and demonstration by Chinese artist Zhang Dan-nung (with arm outstretched), Singapore, 1950

Engagement, Singapore 24 August 1953, with his parents and Margaret's mother (first from left)

Graduation from the University of Malaya, Singapore, with Margaret, 1953

Wedding, London, December 1955

Honeymoon in Torquay at a fancy dress ball, 26 December 1955

At home in Southeast Asia

With Chairman of the Hong Kong Basic Law Drafting Committee Ji Pengfei, 1987

Hong Kong's Executive Council, 9 June 1992, with Governor David Wilson (front row, middle)

Receiving his CBE from Governor David Wilson, Government House, Hong Kong, 13 November 1991

Receiving an Honorary D.Litt. from Sydney University, 18 June 1993

The whole family in Hong Kong, January 1994

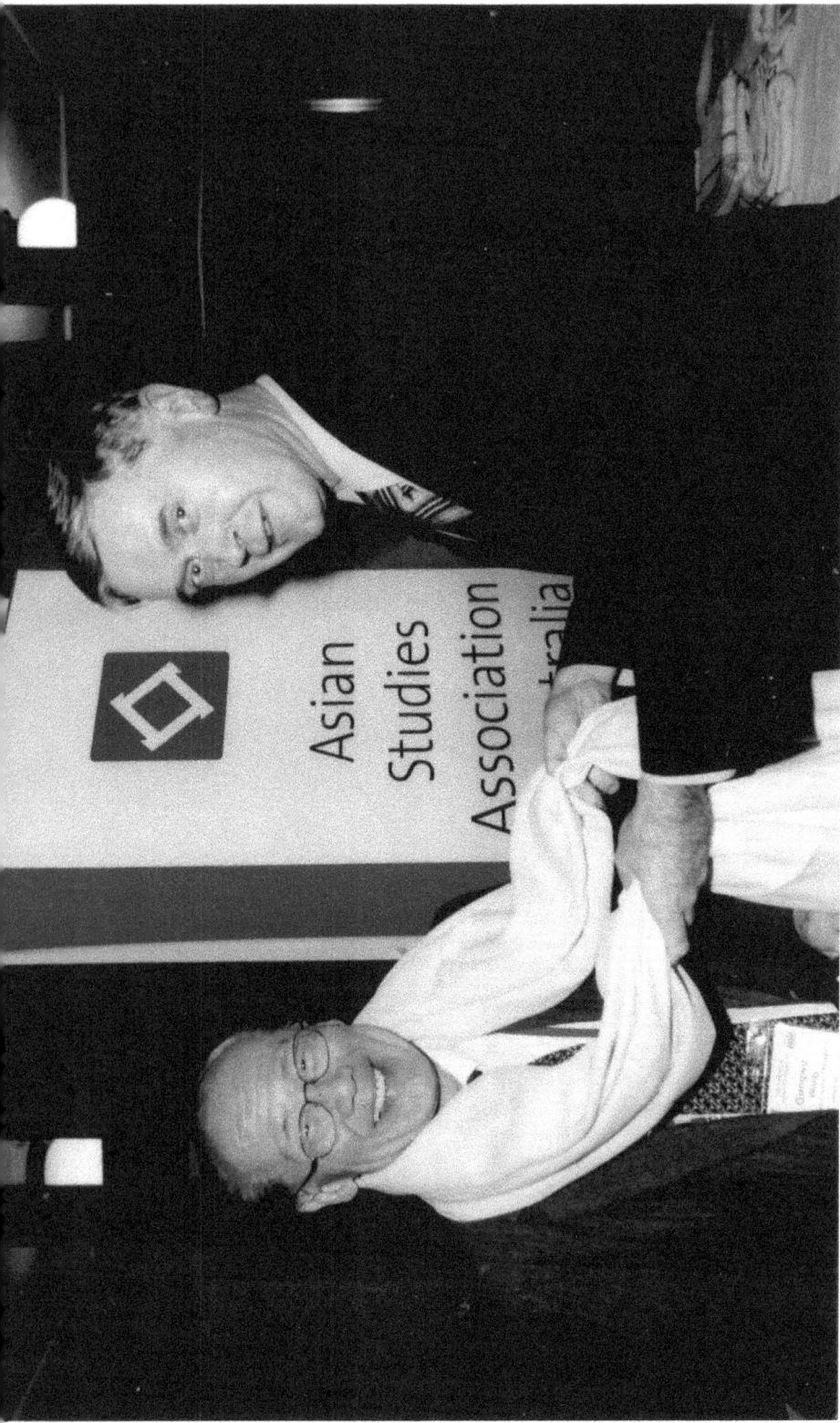

Being felicitated by Robert Cribb in Canberra, 28 June 2004

Having fun in Manila, 1998

Delivering the Daisaku Ikeda Lecture at the Soka Gakkai, 2004

With President S.R. Nathan (centre) and Nobel laureate Sir James Mirrlees, East Asian Institute's 10th Anniversary Dinner, the Istana, Singapore 18 June 2007

www.ingramcontent.com/pod-product-compliance
Lightning Source LLC
Chambersburg PA
CBHW021954090426
42811CB00001B/18